Enneagram Relationships

The Ultimate Guide to Using the Enneagram for Self Discovery

(Remote Work From Home Guide for All Enneagram Types)

Ruben Randle

Published by Knowledge Icons

Ruben Randle

All Rights Reserved

Enneagram Relationships: The Ultimate Guide to Using the Enneagram for Self Discovery (Remote Work From Home Guide for All Enneagram Types)

ISBN 978-1-990084-61-4

All rights reserved. No part of this guide may be reproduced in any form without permission in writing from the publisher except in the case of brief quotations embodied in critical articles or reviews.

Legal & Disclaimer

The information contained in this book is not designed to replace or take the place of any form of medicine or professional medical advice. The information in this book has been provided for educational and entertainment purposes only.

The information contained in this book has been compiled from sources deemed reliable, and it is accurate to the best of the Author's knowledge; however, the Author cannot guarantee its accuracy and validity and cannot be held liable for any errors or omissions. Changes are periodically made to this book. You must consult your doctor or get professional medical advice before using any of the suggested remedies, techniques, or information in this book.

Upon using the information contained in this book, you agree to hold harmless the Author from and against any damages, costs, and expenses, including any legal fees potentially resulting from the application of any of the information provided by this guide. This disclaimer applies to any damages or injury caused by the use and application, whether directly or indirectly, of any advice or information presented, whether for breach of contract, tort, negligence, personal injury, criminal intent, or under any other cause of action.

You agree to accept all risks of using the information presented inside this book. You need to consult a professional medical practitioner in order to ensure you are both able and healthy enough to participate in this program.

Table of Contents

INTRODUCTION 1

CHAPTER 1: THE HISTORY OF THE ENNEAGRAM 4

CHAPTER 2: BENEFIT OF USING ENNEAGRAM 19

CHAPTER 3: THE ENNEAGRAM FAQ 34

CHAPTER 4: TEMPLATE OF PREOCCUPATIONS 44

CHAPTER 5: LEARNING TO TYPE OTHERS 58

CHAPTER 6: TYPE TWO– THE HELPER 67

CHAPTER 7: PHYSICAL APPEARANCE 74

CHAPTER 8: THE LOYALIST SUBTYPES 80

CHAPTER 9: CREATING LEGENDARY LEADERSHIP WITH THE ENNEAGRAM 84

CHAPTER 10: THE HELPER 98

CHAPTER 11: DIFFERENCE BETWEEN THE TYPES OF ENNEAGRAM 109

CHAPTER 12: TYPE TWO – THE HELPER 123

CHAPTER 13: THE ENNEAGRAM PERSONALITY TYPE 5 - THE OBSERVER 145

CHAPTER 14: EFFECTIVE EMPLOYMENT 157

CHAPTER 15: THE INVESTIGATOR 163

CHAPTER 16: TYPE FIVE PERSONALITY............................ 168

CHAPTER 17: TYPE EIGHT: THE IN-CHARGE CAREGIVER . 184

CONCLUSION.. 204

Introduction

Determination of an individual's personality type with the use of the enneagram system does not necessarily put one inside a defined box of nine archetypes. It assists people to see the box from where they are able to experience the world. With this in mind, one can step outside their worldview. Ideally speaking, personality is effective in allowing one to express themselves because they are able to categorize and identify who they really are. At the same time there can be issues when people get stuck in automatic habits. In discovering these unconscious patterns, people are able to lead lives which are more fulfilling and enjoy relationships which are overall healthier. Working within the enneagram model allows people to become successful in their relationships at home and within the working environment. Through understanding automatic reactions and blind spots, people can become more flexible with others in their lives and understand what others are feeling and thinking. This making it easier to tolerate other and be more compassionate. It also helps people to not take the negative reactions or their hostility in such a manner that it is personal. Through the identification of how you are emotionally and psychologically defensive, the enneagram allow you to have a chance at profound growth. At another level it also allows you to develop your relationship with yourself and better this, so that you can become more productive towards yourself and anything within your life.

Simply, the enneagram enables and grows ones capacity when it comes to self-observation. It provides vision for how the healthiest manifestation of people's types can look. Using this detail, it sets a path for the manner in getting to a higher level of awareness. Each type within the enneagram has particular behaviors that satisfy its needs and desires. This is the main strategy of the particular type in life.

That would be driving much of what the type does. The enneagram is able to help people spot when they are being run by their passions, allowing people to satisfy their needs in a healthier manner.

For example, the passion for type seven happens to be gluttony. This is the traditional meaning for overeating which extends to over consumption. The people with this type look for experiences in trying to find a sense of fulfillment which they fear may remain elusive. In truth, they may feel that nothing they embark on will bring the fulfillment which they look for to bring happiness and contentment.

Chapter 1: The History Of The Enneagram

Despite the noise of many self-help professionals have made over the years, very few have been discovered about "self" until the widespread of the knowledge about the all-important tool, the Enneagram. There are many schools of thought that have been developed to facilitate personal discovery, but none of them has been very effective than the Enneagram.

The Enneagram has been accepted globally as the best way to discover yourself and leverage that knowledge towards growth and connection with others. There several articles, webinars and videos that have been published on the subject.

Now, you can start yourself on the road to personal development through the help of the Enneagram of Personality. Through this simple tool, you can discover your gifts, talents, passions, motivations, desires, career path, best match married partner, solve many relationship problems, perform better at work and above all, maximize your potential. Even though the Enneagram seems a little bit complicated, conveyed in simple words and simple terms, you will understand its relevance and how it can radically transform your life. While the diagram might seem confusing and difficult to grasp at first glance, you will love it when you understand what it means and the in-depth insight it provides.

The Origin of The Enneagram

It is also very important that you approach the Enneagram with an open mind, instead of being critical and judgmental about its history, origin, and theories. To fully embrace the Enneagram and appreciate the beauty, you need to understand its origin and history.

The origin of the Enneagram has been inundated with debates, arguments and various points of views. Notwithstanding, all schools of thoughts have somewhat agreed that the origin of the Enneagram symbol stems from ancient great philosophers, the work of Pythagoras and religions such as Christianity, Judaism, Buddhism, Islam, and Hinduism, that traced back into antiquity.

In the work and teachings of George Ivanovich Gurdjieff, he used the symbol to represent sacred dances and movements in the universe. He was the first person who started using the symbol to refer to a person's chief ego. He referred to points around the circle as a person's "chief feature." In an attempt to educate the students to the essence of the symbol, Gurdjieff employed the Sufi tradition to explain how vile people could be.

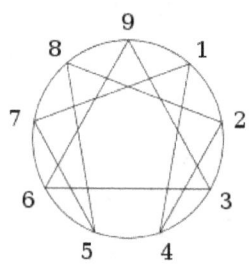

Figure 1: Enneagram Figure

The modern Enneagram and its related meaning have been known as the creative work of Oscar Ichazo. Other historians revealed that Ichazo was one of the students of Gurdjieff and might have learned the symbol and some of the core interpretation from his master. Having been intrigued with the Enneagram symbol, he set out to dig deeper and find more knowledge on how the symbol can be used to understand the human personality.

As a scholar and a researcher, his consistent studies to understand the human personality led him to the discovery of nine vices and virtues of the human soul. These negative and positive qualities of the human soul were further incorporated into the "Gurdjieff 9-pointed process diagram." Further studies related to Arica that each point on the diagram stands for human personality type. He used a numerical symbol to represent each of them.

After a thorough work on Enneagram, Ichazo decided to establish a school to teach the personality types and how it relates to the Enneagram symbol. In the 1970s, the Arica Institute was formed in Arica, Chile to help people discover who they are, and how they can best use the Enneagram symbol for self-discovery, self-mastery, and spiritual growth.

Arica Institute was focused on teaching people a system of "inner work" to help them transform their human consciousness. Some of the subjects taught in relation to "inner work" included spirituality, psychology, metaphysics, and cosmetology.

In the book, Personality Types, where Ichazo was interviewed to provide clarifications to the vices and virtues in the diagram, he said the following words: "An essential individual will be in contact with these [Virtues] constantly, simply by living in his body. But the subjective individual, the ego, loses touch with these virtues.

Then the personality tries to compensate by developing passions."

Claudia Naranjo and John Lilly, renowned psychologists and writers were some of the students of the school. After leaving Chile for the United States, Claudia began to teach the Enneagram of Personality based on his own insight and interpretation. Many people including some Jesuit priests in the United States began to adopt the Enneagram of Personality for Christian counseling and spiritual development.

Other students of the Enneagram such as Helen Palmer, Don Richard Riso, Richard Rohr, and Elizabeth Wagele began writing and publishing books about the Enneagram of Personality in the 1980s and 1990s. Since then, the Ennagram of Personality has been expanded and developed to help people in all fields of life to use. Lately, apps and websites have been developed to provide personality tests to people after answering a series of questions.

The Enneagram of Personality Structure

To know how the Enneagram works, you have to first and foremost grasp a basic understanding of the modern-day Enneagram. Even though the Enneagram seem complicated from a first impression when you understand it, you will be mesmerized by its simplicity and embraced how it can actually enable you to gain a deeper knowledge of who you are and how to relate well with others.

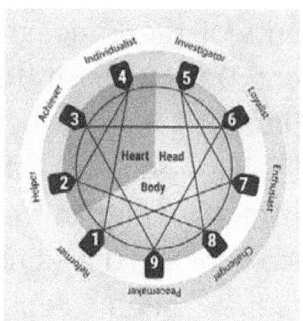

Figure 2: The Enneagram of Personality

Enneagram, pronounced "any-a-gram", comes from two Greek words: "Ennea" means nine and "gram" means "something written or drawn." It literally means "a nine-pointed diagram". Basically, it is a star-shaped drawing in a circle made up of nine equidistant points connected together by intersecting lines. Each point on the geometric shape is used to refer to a personality type with associated vices and virtues.

In those days, for people to understand themselves and gain self-discovery of their personality, they had to visit their priest for counseling and spiritual direction. Through the extensive work of Ichazo and other fellows, the Enneagram tool can be used by the average person with the help of an Enneagram coach to gain a deeper insight to various personality types and how they relate to each other.

It is very important that you understand that the whole purpose of Enneagram is to understand the subconscious motivations that guide and directs people to behave in the natural world. It helps to understand a person's approach and perspective to life without their foreknowledge. By understanding an individual's core personality, the knowledge gained can be used for further personal growth.

How the Enneagram of Personality Structure Works

The Intelligence Centre: The intelligence center is made up of the body (instinct/action), heart (feeling) and the head (thinking). These three triads of intelligence play a critical role in the formation and development of each personality type. Each personality type is designated with a number with a name given to each based on predisposed qualities, attitudes, and behaviors.

Ichazo realized when a person is born into this world; they come with a pure essence that is not diluted in any way. In order words, we were all born with the fairly, innocent and purely image which is built into the human soul. But through the formative stages of life, before we turn to age seven (7), environmental factors begin to affect our thinking (head), feeling (heart) and gut instincts (body) which further determines the way we each behave and conduct ourselves.

The Personality Types: Based on the environmental, social and genetic factors that play a critical role in the formative stages of a person, a particular personality type will be developed. According to the Enneagram model, the behavioral patterns developed by people due to variation in their thinking, feeling and action are what leads to the different personality types.

The following enlists the nine personality types of the Enneagram and how they each approach life:

●Type One: Reformer/Perfectionist—I need to do everything right and perfect.

●Type Two: Helper/Giver—I need to help other people.

●Type Three: Achiever/ Motivator /Performer—I need to succeed and do exploits.

●Type Four: Individualistic /Artistic/Romantic- I need to be authentic and exploit my uniqueness.

- Type Five: Investigator / Observer/Thinker—I need to understand everything and know "why".
- Type Six: Loyalist/Skeptic/Questioner—I need to be wary of people.
- Type Seven: Enthusiastic / Generalist/Epicure- I am always open to new opportunities.
- Type Eight: Challenger/Warrior/Boss— I need to be courageous and strong.
- Type Nine: Peacemaker/Mediator—I need to be at peace with others.

The Vices/Virtues of Each Personality Type: Each personality type on the diagram is not better than the other. They all have strengths and weaknesses. The weaknesses are what people are likely to express when they are under stressful situations. In those low points of life, the "vices" of their dominant personality expresses itself and causes them to behave in a way they should not.

The vices are referred to us as "deadly sins." For example, even though the Giver has a genuine urge to give, he can exhibit pride and begin to brag about his acts of generosity to other people.

The perfectionist is likely to get angry with other people or things when things are not as perfect as he wants them to be. These are the "deadly sins" or "vices" associated with that personality.

How the Enneagram Personality Types Interact

You see, the daily behavior and habits of people are driven by unconscious motives and intentions. These hidden motives are what makes them do what they do, enter a specific career and connect with people in a particular way. The emotional drives, then, creates a way of handling, approaching and dealing with the everyday affairs of life.

When you know your personality, and that of other people, it will enable you to accept people just as they are without any criticism. It will also develop empathy for people and connect with them in a way that brings understanding and harmony. In fact, it will dramatically impact your overall outlook and relationship in every sphere of life.

The Wings: It is very important to understand that each personality type in the Enneagram model is not better than the other. Each personality type has its virtue and vices which makes it unique. Another key thing to know is that people are complicated and cannot be put in a box.

The diagram is simply a road map to guide you towards self-discovery and not a tool to limit you as a person. You can't just say that a fellow is Type One and that's all. In most cases, you may have a core personality type with one or two other types which complement the core/basic personality type.

The other personality types, which in a way, alter your basic type are known as the "wings." The wing-type personalities serve a complement to the dominant personality. This is the reason there are lines connecting the personality types on the Enneagram. This is to show that most people are likely to have a combination of types (core/dominant type and a wing-type) which blends to form their overall personality.

For example, a person with a Type Eight as a core is likely to have Type Two and Type One as a wing type. This is because most leaders have a strong urge to achieve, perform and accomplish their goals, and they try to make sure that everything is perfect.

All these personality types operate in them in tandem, not exclusive of each other.

one, two or even three wings. For some people, the other wing types are dark and unnoticeable. The development of other wings is due to the emotional development that a person goes through as he/she goes through life. Due to the circumstances of life, other wing types are formed, developed and added to the core personality type. This is how the Enneagrams interact with each other and complement each other.

The key is to first and foremost discover your dominant personality type and then look at which other wings you possess. Also remember that even though you may have a wing personality which will complement the core personality type, your feeling, thinking, and actions will be mostly dominated by the core/basic personality. The best way to understand yourself is to study and read the descriptions of other personality types and then see how it fits into your overall personality.

Chapter 2: Benefit Of Using Enneagram

The most important benefit that the Enneagram provides is that it will help you to understand yourself. It will help you to understand your inner self. It will also help you to understand others. When you understand others, you can be more compassionate towards them. The Enneagram will help you to not just access, but even expand your emotional, mental, and spiritual intelligence. You will be aware of your automatic responses and defensive reactions towards situations in life. When you are aware of the manner in which you react, you can change your reactions. The only thing that you can fully control in your life is your reactions. The difference between success and failure is your reaction. The way you react can decide the course of your life. Thus, the Enneagram will improve your efficiency when you interact with others. Not just that, it will help you to build meaningful relationships. It will help you to live in the present and not the past or the future. Well, it all boils down to self-awareness. Being aware of yourself will help you to change your life for the better.

Confidence

The eighth, and second to last personality that we will look at in this book is called the challenger. They are named this because they never turn down challenges. It is more like they feed on these challenges. Challengers are quick to make decisions and have high confidence in the choices that they make. This confidence has earned them the nicknames of Willful, Powerful and Self-confident. They always feel the need to control the environment because of their surety. Because of this, they have also known for being quite dominating.

Influential and inspirational but sometimes becomes intimidating; people of the eighth personality do not like to show weakness. They would rather challenge those around them in order to show their resourcefulness and skill. They never miss a chance at turning a challenge into a means to better them. They make advances at taking control before anyone else has an opportunity even to try let alone acquiring any form of rule over them. They fear to be vulnerable and possibly being hurt or dominated by others.

There is no way around it challengers are highly competitive people. They will do anything to win and ensure that the perceived opponent has no advantage over them. They feel a need to win at everything, and revel in their strengths, abilities, and work. They not only dislike human control, but they also hate being controlled by circumstances. Much like the seventh personality we looked at, challengers do not like feeling restricted. Sometimes these two personalities are mistaken for one another. This is especially true when an eighth's dominant wing is a seven, or a seven's dominant wing is an eight.

No matter how much contradiction challengers face, they only want to do what seems right to them and would go to any length to achieve their goals. Unlike the seventh personality that goes to extremes in order to get what they want because of a need for excitement, challengers go to extremes because they want to prove their worth and show their strength. They don't mind being forced out of their comfort zones because they like the idea that they have the opportunity to give more than they usually do and be even better than they already are.

Self-Awareness

Now that you have discovered your personality type, it is important that you consider actions and steps that will allow you the joys of personal growth to become more self-aware. As you would guess, different personalities have different actions and recommendations for the journey of self-awareness. Therefore, let us examine each of these individually in order to help you identify what works best for your type.

Benefit of Self-Awareness

Your coping skills will improve

Life will always throw challenges at you. When you lack self-awareness, you may address obstacles from a place of reactivity, and it becomes much harder to cope. With awareness, you can handle these difficulties from a place of grace and acceptance, and it becomes easier to remain positive and relaxed, and to make empowering choices.

You will heal yourself.

When pain remains buried and unaddressed, hurt lingers on in your body, making you more likely to react to the present from the place of your past pain. Working through your challenges makes it easier to act consciously and frees you from the burdens you carry. People tend to feel much better each time an issue gets resolved.

Your internal sense of balance will increase.

Sometimes, you may feel as if you are on an emotional tightrope. Each emotion and reaction has the potential to hit you like a strong gust of wind, leaving you struggling to cling to the delicate balance you've created. Self-awareness gives you strength, and acceptance makes you even stronger. You can maintain your balance and weather internal storms.

Your relationships will get better.

You can make it easy for others to enjoy your company when you relate to them from a place of awareness. When you react to others from a place of unconsciousness, you have more conflicts, and greater hurt may arise in relationships. With self-awareness, you develop compassion for others' pain. It is easier to connect with others from a place of kindness.

You will develop presence and mindfulness.

Being present allows people to live in the here and now. When we are focused on only the current moment, we don't need to feel hurt by the wounds from the past or fear the unknown in the future. We find acceptance and joy in everything. We simply are. In presence, we see others and ourselves fully and compassionately.

Compassion

The enneagram allows for one to get on a journey towards self-enlightenment and acceptance for who you are. Everyone has a basic driving force and a preferred strategy set for unique talents and strengths that make us individuals. We look at the world and the present era with specific perspectives and we are drawn in particular directions as individuals. These preferences can harden into modes of behavior, which also strangle the ways in which we grow. At times when people first discover the particular type they are, they might say that they would like to change to another type. That is an indication they are judging one type to be more desirable as compared to another. The key to utilizing the enneagram would be exploration without the use of judgment. The question is if each pattern provided a large reservoir of talent, which is equally valuable. You are undoubtedly growing and maturing everyday so there should not be a limit to the potentials irrespective of your type. Every evidence points to the fact that no enneagram type is better than the other. In each archetype there are different levels of maturity and generativity. The level of maturity may vary though in different contexts.

Each type of enneagram represents a deep habit. It shows a theme that for a lot of people is constant throughout their life, though the possibilities for the mental, physical or spiritual developments have no bounds. The type is a fundamental form of human habit. With some technology and coaching, it is possible to utilize the information gained from this information to transform patterns for more effective behavior and perspectives.

As we study our types, it begins to dawn on us that there is a range of healthy to unhealthy behaviors we engage in unwittingly. When we are relaxed, we may feel safe and have natural gifts that are inherent to our type that are at our disposal. Similarly, when under stress, we have ways of reacting that may run contrary to the best intentions we have. When triggered we may also react in the best way to protect ourselves from pain, fear or shame and respond so quickly that we do not even acknowledge the effect that it has on other people. When growing to understand our type, we develop the right skills which are particular to that type and that may allow us to reduce the levels of stress we harbor through reactivity and our quick responses which negatively affect the ones that are around us. This also allows the illustration of the greatest gifts and as we continue to learn, there is an understanding that others also have unconscious patterns and reactions which are predictable during times of crises, happening beyond the level of present awareness.

With more study, one may start to develop valuable traits such as compassion and understanding for themselves and others concerning the patterns of the type and then grow to appreciate just how fast anyone can be triggered and how much it is not possible to note the patterns. Develop skills that would slow things down and bring us out of the trance that instilled patterns we engage. We can then become compassionate and sensitive to the emotional vulnerabilities of everyone and become skilled at holding space for them. Under stress, each category has a way they disconnect from their loved ones emotionally.

In depth exploration concerning the enneagram also assists one to navigate their relationships with more skill. Knowing the types of your family and colleagues can increase your understanding on their fears, defenses and motivations, allowing you to understand how they would interact with you and others. The other reason you should take this journey into self-exploration is the commitment to living a conscious and caring life though every day you may come across situations and people that could result in self-sabotaging reactions. Even if you had been on a spiritual path for some time, you may still be humbled by the manner that the unconscious reactions bring you to patterns that you had thought had been outgrown.

It could be that you tend to space when your spouse expresses painful emotions because it disrupts your carefree attitude, or you may turn to alcohol or other drugs when you feel like you are being shunned or things are not going your way. Irrespective of the pattern, everyone comes with habits that block self-expression and joy. All of these patterns which are negative because of their own suffering and they are linked to habits of the different enneagram types. Even in the event that you can recite deep spiritual truths when these patterns are triggered, you may still forget the bigger picture of who you are and the unique gifts that you can share with the world. The question then arises on how one can find clarity and free themselves from the fears, motivations and desires that fuel behavioral patterns and trigger other reactions from others.

Leadership

People who fit into the challenger category are both convincing and charismatic. Hence, they can be found in a variety of leadership positions. They tend to be the best in their different fields and can sometimes be seen as paragons of whatever it is they stand for. Because of their ability to exercise so much control and restraint, they significantly affect their society and believe they have a full understanding of how things should work. They expect that everyone follows them and will fight opposition at all costs. They also have powerful instincts that they'll follow at all costs rather than go along with someone else's or being convinced to ignore their instincts.

Much like people of the sixth personality, trust is not an easy thing to achieve for challengers, but when they do realize it, they make that person into a very close friend and give that person a level of importance in their lives. People of the eighth personality begin to use their protective instincts to defend these people who are close to them and would do anything to provide for those people.

Challengers do not appreciate any form of control over them. They fear allowing external factors to influence them and will fight no matter what to break that influence. They choose to always grow their power, resources, and skills, which puts them way ahead of any threats of being overthrown. They are the most independent of all the types of personalities of the Enneagram.

Challengers might listen to advice from others, but they ensure they have the final say. They like to make sure they and no one else is the decision maker in their lives. Because of this, they often have problems with hierarchy if they aren't at the top. They often come off as rebellious because they are so strong-willed and feel a need for their opinions to heard and acknowledged.

When it comes to fears and concerns, people of this personality fear physical harm. But their primary fear is the feeling of being vulnerable in any way. Sometimes, challengers find intimate relationships hard to participate in because it requires a level of vulnerability, and people of this personality do not like to open up. This, combined with a fear of betrayal, also makes it difficult for challengers to engage in intimate relationships with anyone. It's not like they are entirely unfeeling. They have sentimental sides but would rather keep those sites hidden so that no one can see them as vulnerable or see those sentiments as an opportunity to gain control over them.

People well known in their various fields or groups are most likely perfect examples of challengers. People such as Donald Trump, Queen Latifah, Serena Williams, Pablo Picasso, and Franklin Roosevelt, Ernest Hemingway, James Brown, Pink, Jack Black, and Humphrey Bogart all fit into this category.

Chapter 3: The Enneagram Faq

Now that we have explored briefly the evolution and origins of the Enneagram, our journey toward defining our personality can begin. The idea of Enneagram personality raises a number of questions that stem from misunderstanding and lack of reliable information. Before you learn more about nine personality types and how you can use them to understand yourself and others, this chapter will provide answers to frequently asked questions. This way, you will get more insight and understanding of the subject and a stronger foundation for important lessons that Enneagram can teach you.

How can I find out my Enneagram personality type?

The first question that comes to your mind is, most likely, how to find out your personality type. You have different options depending on your preferences and budget. Probably the best place to start learning about the Enneagram is through books like this one. In order to truly understanding your personality type and how it can help you, it's important to get educated about the Enneagram itself. The greatest advantage of learning about the Enneagram personality types is the opportunity to learn at your own pace, you don't have to keep up with anyone which is a great thing if you have a busy schedule on a daily basis. Besides books, you can also consider signing up for the Enneagram class or workshop. With the increasing popularity of this tradition, it's easy to find the nearest workshop, just type the keywords (the Enneagram workshop + your location) in Google search and you'll get plenty of options.

In addition to the workshops and books, it is practical to consider guidance and services from someone who's into the ancient personality types method. These individuals have a thorough understanding of this tradition and they can help you identify your personality type easily. The internet offers plenty of resources too, but you should be cautious because not all websites are equal and some of them provide inaccurate information.

Bear in mind that identifying one's personality type can be a confusing experience, especially if you lack experience. Don't expect to learn everything in a day. Take it slow and always remember that consistency and willpower are essential here. Give yourself some time to learn and gain experience, it will be easier for you to identify your personality type when you avoid pushing yourself or feeling bad because of a slower pace than expected. One of the most common culprits to why identifying personality type is confusing or frustrating is down to the fact that types are determined by patterns that tend to be unconscious to the individual. That's why these patterns are difficult to recognize. The Enneagram urges you to get to know your internal patterns of behavior, thinking, or emotions in order to compare them to descriptions of different types.

Your true personality type lies in knowing yourself.

Is the Enneagram related to the Myers-Briggs Type Indicator (MBTI)?

If you're familiar with the MBTI, you've probably wondered whether the Enneagram correlates to this personality type indicator. This is a complex subject, but essentially there is no proven correlation between the two methods. Anyway, it is important to mention that a few comparisons showed some Enneagram groups match MBTI types with higher frequency and degree than other MBTI types. This is probably the biggest reason why the Enneagram is oftentimes compared to the MBTI, but there is no reliable data showing this comparison is consistent or that it applies to a larger population. Basically, even if there is a match between the two, it only occurs on rare occasions and applies to the smaller fraction of people. Plus, their core is different. While the Enneagram focused on a person's habits of emotions, attention, feelings, and similar thought patterns the MBTI pays more attention to other mental functions. What we can conclude here that although these two personality indicators are compared with one another, they use a different approach to identify an individual's personality type.

Can I be more than one personality type?

You know how you belong to one zodiac sign, but you also have an ascendant? The human psyche is too complex to be boxed in a specific definition and it is natural to wonder whether you can have more than personality types in the Enneagram too. Every person poses as a fusion of all nine personality types. Even though you will have patterns that correspond to some other personality type, there is only one that domains over all others. More precisely, although our patterns of behavior, thinking, and emotions are a combination of all nine types, there is always one personality type that prevails i.e. it's your core point.

The patterns of our inner thoughts or emotions represent the manner you respond to different circumstances. As you're already aware, you don't react to some situations, in the same way, all the time. Sometimes you even change the way you respond to different circumstances within the same day. Throughout your lifetime, you can manifest all or some specific Enneagram personality types, but one of these patterns is constant and it occurs more often than any other. Therefore, while you may experience patterns of behavior corresponding to different Enneagram types throughout your life, you only have one dominant personality type.

Do we ever change dominant personality type?

Okay, now that we have established each individual has one dominant personality type, it seems natural to wonder if there is really a possibility to change the core point during a lifetime. The short answer is no, but I'm going to elaborate it for a better understanding of the subject. The patterns that define your personality type are rooted in your psyche, dominate behaviors and experiences throughout your life. That's why it's important to know yourself and the way you think, behave, feel or respond to different circumstances in order to truly understand the importance of the Enneagram and its meaning.

What is a subtype?

According to the Enneagram tradition, each personality has three subtypes. The subtypes are social, sexual, and self-preservation. It is important to mention that all nine personality types in the Enneagram have these three subtypes. A social subtype is associated with our relationship to groups while sexual is implicated with our reactions regarding one-to-one relationships. Lastly, self-preservation refers to survival issues and meeting the needs to survive. Of course, one of these subtypes dominates over the others in each person.

Can I be compatible with some specific personality type?

We're always looking to associate ourselves with people who are compatible to us thinking that's the key to a strong and healthy relationship. Since understanding the Enneagram helps you improve the relationship with others, one thing that people frequently ask is whether we can be compatible with certain personality type, similar to the zodiac. The answer to this question is both yes and no.

Yes in a way that different personality types can share common characteristics like One with a Two wing. At the same time, the answer is no because all healthy individuals are compatible with one another regardless of their personality type. It is a commonly accepted theory that any two types that are adjacent to one another on the circle e.g. One and Two, relate well together. Although it's a common practice to theorize whether some personality types are compatible, there is no research or any evidence that describes tendencies of some personality types toward others.

What is a wing?

The term wing refers to the Enneagram point that is on either side of and immediately adjacent to your core point. For example, type Four has two wings: Three and Five. What does this mean? It means that in some circumstances the core characteristics of that personality type will be influenced by those linked with Three and Five types.

What is the best Enneagram type?

Although you've probably thought this way, the significance of the Enneagram isn't to pit people against one another or to claim you have to be a certain type in order to feel valued. One personality type is not better or worse than the other. They are different, but it's not a bad thing – that's the beauty of it. After all, the Enneagram shows that all those nine different personalities make a perfect circle. You shouldn't change yourself to fit one Enneagram type, primarily because it stems from internal patterns of behavior.

Chapter 4: Template Of Preoccupations

Now we come to the template of preoccupations of the types. In this section I present a list of concerns for each personality type. You may see some of these traits in yourself or someone you are deeply connected with. They certainly will help you discover in what areas your current breakdowns lie in.

Type 1: The Perfectionist

Enneagram type 1 is known to be critical of themselves and others. The have a tendency for strong self-criticism, and usually have a "top dog" mentality

They judge themselves against their own standards of right and wrong. They even ignore others' standards.

They demonstrate what it means to be correct and responsible. If you need something done, assigning the task to a one will usually work well.

Their preoccupation with perfection compels them to compare themselves with others.

Ones fall into the habit of being "good boy" and "good girl".

In order to achieve perfection, they sometimes procrastinate until they feel that they are right. Being right is extremely important, so they try and try to get it right. They cannot handle failure very well.

This makes them vulnerable to falling into an emotional trap door, which they have difficulty getting out of. They are trapped by their necessity to be right and perfect and at the same time, wanting to be the good person and get results.

Ones like their independence and prefer to have things go their way. They think that virtue is its own reward.

Now get them involved in a righteous cause and they can be real dynamos. They will take on responsibility for large projects and do them exceedingly well. Their fixation on anger makes them productive in these situations.

Type 2: The Giver

The giver is more concerned with people and relationships than anything else in his or her life. They take pride in what they can do for you, ignoring their own needs. The needs of others come before their own.

This focus of attention on others is characterized by an outstanding ability to selectively merge with people and their problems and concerns. They are able to provide excellent feedback to people in need, and they can easily share in the joys and triumphs of others.

In a similar vein, twos neurotically alter to please everyone. They can present a different personality to their best friends, children and spouse. This manifests in their ability to change in order to please someone and get their love.

Pride is the fixation of the two. They take pride in their ability to meet your needs. This helping of others is also a means of getting affection.

Try to give a gift to a two and you will find that they have a difficult time receiving it. [I know this from personal experience. My wife is a two and it is almost impossible to please her with a gift, especially clothing or jewelry. I have learned to give her massages or restorative yoga classes, instead.]

You have to watch out for a two in case the sell you out for approval from someone important to them.

Twos are the type of people that move towards other people. This is a coping strategy defined by Karen Horney. See points eight and five for the other neurotic coping strategies.

In this way, their attention is on the other and their quest for freedom makes it certain that one person is not enough!

Type 3: The Performer

Vanity, being the fixation of point three on the enneagram, makes threes over concerned with their image and achievement. They are task oriented and can utilize polyphasic thinking to get a lot of jobs done, and done exceptionally well.

Even their leisure time is task oriented. Trips must be planned to the exact moment and the places they go must be top drawer!

Winning is the only thing that counts. They can become "supermoms" and step on others to get their tasks done.

Their image is all important and it can be real or fantasy. Deluded threes live in this fantasy world where appearances are all important.

Vanity and deceit characterize their feelings, especially when it comes to performance and living for the eyes of others.

Type 4: The Romantic

Envy is the fixation of type four on the enneagram. This envy comes from their feeling of loss and longing to have what others have. This gives rise to feelings of depression, melancholy and sadness.

One of the primary characteristics of type four is the intensity of their feelings. The feel everything quite strongly and are attracted to melancholy.

Because of this intensity of feelings, they are masters of empathy and are good around others when others are depressed.

Their deep emotionality gives the appearance of authenticity. This makes them either depressed or active.

Fours are often fashion oriented, and you will see them in all kinds of fancy getups. This provides them with the feeling of being special.

Type 5: The Observer

Stinginess is the fixation of point five on the enneagram. This greed is primarily for their strong privacy needs. They like to be in the background and control everything from their ivory tower.

Another aspect of their greed is the reduction of needs, which makes them stingy and hoard what they have.

They feel that other people are intrusive into their space and they want it all for themselves.

This type of avoidance of people is especially noticeable when it comes to small talk and cocktail parties. Fives avoid them like the plague!

The fives seem to relish in their secret lives, all compartmentalized to meet their own needs. This gives them the "moving away" classification on Karen Horney's scale of coping styles.

Fives use magical thinking to ward off intrusion and disturbances. They often pretend to not hear anything, when in reality, they have heard every word!

In order to maintain their privacy and guard their space, the always prepare for what they have to do.

They keep their knowledge to themselves, especially knowledge about themselves. They have a difficult time sharing themselves with other people.

For fives, the time they spend with their own thoughts is precious. Hanging out with people on distracts them from their favorite activity of acquiring knowledge.

The five likes to stay invisible, so they manage from the back office and let subordinates appear to run the show.

Watch out for those fives, as they are very sensitive to intrusions into their privacy, for which they are constantly scanning.

It is in their private space that they can only begin to feel their feelings, and these are often quite vague.

In a lot of ways, fives are detached people. They don't meddle in other people's affairs and don't feel a need to consume much goods and services.

Because of this, they are self-sufficient, maybe too much so.

They may be hiding behind their fear of feeling things or their fear of being in relationships.

On the positive side, fives are often calm when other are not – probably a result of detachment. They are also precise with works and language.

Type 6: The Trooper

Other names for point six on the enneagram are the loyalist or loyal skeptic.

Helen Palmer originally called this point the devil's advocate.

In any case, there are two types of sixes: phobic and counter phobic.

The phobic sixes are flooded with self-doubt and fear and they fail to taken action because of the fear.

The counter phobic sixes are not at all afraid to do dangerous activities. They are, in fact, motivated by fear.

Both types if sixes have authority issues. They either cow down to authority or they completely ignore it.

Scanning for harm and danger is a characteristic of all sixes. They like to sit with their backs to a wall in a restaurant so they can scan the environment.

Sixes are constantly checking people out and detecting their bullshit.

Some sixes procrastinate because they are afraid. The fear causes a paralysis when it comes to getting things done.

Often, successful sixes begin to doubt their success. This leads to self-sabotage of their careers.

Projection of doubt and fear cause an increase in these qualities. The fear can be real or imaginary.

On the other hand, sixes like to undertake underdog causes. This is because when they get behind a cause, they become loyal, perform their duty, and display a quality of self-sacrifice.

Many sixes like to find a trustworthy protector so they can feel secure.

When looking to future, a six often sees the worst case scenario. This gives rise to their devil's advocate position.

Type 7: The Epicure

The fixation of point seven on the enneagram is planning. All plans lead to fun!

Sevens always like to have multiple options going at a time.

They are excellent at reframing an otherwise negative situation.

Sevens have a fascination for all the good things in life, and they are able to process many things at once.

They get involved in lots of projects but may not complete any of them. Thus they are good starters.

Sevens would rather have great experiences than success, although their personality is usually happy and optimistic.

Sevens are often overbooked, sometimes to escape pain. For them, life is an adventure and the world is their goal.

They think themselves superior to others, when, in fact, they may be inferior. This is their mechanism for rationalization.

Type 8: The Boss

The fixation of point eight on the enneagram is vengeance. Eights must be in control at all times. Anyone who steps on their authority is met with a vengeance.

Eights are usually quite competent, and the get angry very easily.

They admire people who confront and oppose them. They think these types of people are trustworthy and not a "yes person."

For eights, the truth is very important – more so than agreement.

As friends, bosses and lovers, eights enjoy fighting the battles of others.

For eights, it's hostile out there and it is okay to break the rules to get what you want.

They are passionate, lustful people and they have the capacity to take in a lot. This, however, leads to excess in all areas of life: food, drink, sex, relationships, and everything else.

Type 9: The Mediator

Type nine on the enneagram tends to be indolent in terms of their own spiritual and emotional progress.

They would rather merge with the wishes of others, almost indiscriminately.

Others opinions are more important than their own and their energy often comes from others.

This is because nine have the uncanny ability to see all sides of an issue.

They control by means of passive aggression.

When they are in the service of others, they have a strong ability to stay on track.

Their anger is reflected by stubbornness in an effort to contain their anger.

Nines behavior can often be quite pleasing and caring, and they have a difficult time saying no.

They like structure, peace and tranquility, not decisions.

Nines can get totally involved with inessential things and ignore the essential.

Their indolence makes them slow to accumulate things, especially for themselves. If you tell them to do something for their own good, they will procrastinate by finding inessential activites.

Chapter 5: Learning To Type Others

The teachings of G.I. Gurdjieff and Oscar Ichazo have much to do with the Enneagram gaining as much prominence as it has in recent decades. Ichazo and Gurdjieff were teaching far away from each other, using different methods and languages, but their common interest of helping people to become their deepest authentic selves through a program of inner work. Gurdjieff worked and lived in Russia and then France. Ichazo established a school in Arica, Chile in the 1960's, where he taught his way of using the Enneagram for self-analysis.

Gurdjieff was the one who connected a Platonic-inflected conception of essence versus form in his teachings. He taught that one had both an essence and a personality. The essence of a person is their nature; it is some inherent truth of their being. It is the nature of a person. The personality is what has arisen from the context and circumstances that we grow up and develop with. The way to finding one's essential self, to Gurdjieff, was spending time in a rigorous program of observing oneself, and that we all individually and collectively need to strive for transformation to evolve.

Oscar Ichazo is largely responsible for the Enneagram system of personality that most people work with today. Ichazo initially labeled the system of self-analysis used to work with the Enneagram as "protoanalysis". He had one particularly bright student named Claudio Naranjo. Naranjo studied with Ichazo and he carried over Ichazo's teachings to Berkeley, California in the early 70's. Naranjo led groups of people participating in protoanalysis, and taught about the personality types. Naranjo was born in Chile but had trained in the United States as a psychiatrist. He took many different perspectives into consideration in his development and teachings, including Jungian archetypes, the work of Karen Horney, existential philosophy, psychoanalysis, and the work of G.I. Gurdjieff. The Enneagram struck him as a powerful tool for personal growth and an integrative model of personality.

The teachings of Gurdjieff, Ichazo, and Naranjo fall into several different categories of study. Some have suggested the term "psycho-spiritual", that is, addressing problems of both psychology and spirituality. When we compare the psycho-spiritual system of teachings presented by Gurdjieff, Ichazo, and Naranjo to psychoanalysis, we see a great number of similarities. Both theories of the Enneagram and psychoanalytic theory view personality as a result of the interaction of a child with the world. They both want to take into account the child's innate disposition and the child's environment. One difference is that psychoanalytic theory focuses a little more on childhood, and the Enneagram is applicable equally to children and adults.

Fr. Richard Rohr is an American Franciscan friar who was ordained into the priesthood in 1970. Rohr is partly responsible for framing the Enneagram and its wisdom into a Christian perspective. He wrote a book in 1995 which brought the Enneagram into the spotlight for many Catholics. At this time, the Enneagram was introduced to a wider audience as a tool for spirituality.

There is a holistic quality to the Enneagram system of personality. It directs our attention to the tripartheid division that we all experience in the head, head, the heart, and the body. This is mirrored in the intellect, emotion, and behavior. The Enneagram supports an equal consideration of body and mind, as often seen to non-western philosophy. The Enneagram supports a balance of these three for functioning.

When using the Enneagram to distinguish which Type you associate most closely to, you want to consider some different elements of the Enneagram's map of personality. The Enneagram makes some distinctions in categories: the gut, the hart, and the head types. These correlate to sexual drives, social drives, and self-preserving drives.

So what le now, an important part of considering the Enneagram and unlocking these personality types to better understand others and improve communication is that each person is a microcosm of the whole system. That is to say that all nine types think, feel, have a sex drive, a drive for self-perseveration, and social impulses. All nine types have strengths and faults. So in parsing your own type and other personality types, you must remain conscious of the common attitudes that we have, and also the contextual factors for personality. Betty, in the office, may only be showing you one side of her that will lead you to think she's a Protector. But in most of her life, she is the Loyalist. When she is challenged to an extreme, she behaves like The Investigator. We may embody many different aspects of each of the personalities, but if you were able to look closer into Betty's life, you'd see that she has core attitudes and developmental tendencies that align with the drives of one type.

What leads us to our most core personality type? People have to survive in the world! We start to organize traits and characterizes that will let us make our way and form relationships, with others and ourselves. Personality is mad up of our defense mechanisms, habits of thought, the emotions that come with the thoughts, interpersonal aptitudes and abilities, and a way of physicality to manifest our energy. Once we understand our tendency to have one way of living, we can unlock the opportunity for proactive, rather than reactive behavior.

The Triads, wings, and variants of the Enneagram model can provide even further insight into our behaviors and tendencies. Both of the types on either side of any given Enneagram type are the wings of that type. People are never always one of the personalities described in the Enneagram; they are always a combination of one or two of them. This is one reason why no two people ever seem completely alike in their behavior. If an individual is mainly a Type Three, the wings of Type Three will also be present in their behavior and personality. This means that sometimes they may embody the characteristics of a Type Two, and sometimes they may imitate a Type Four. Some will say that an individual draws equally from both wings, that is, if they are a Type One, that they derive equal influence from each of their wings. Others think that people tend to characterize the influence from only one wing at a time.

Let's discuss the secure and stress embodiments of each of the types. The Enneagram's lines illustrate an individual's shift in personality when they are facing security, versus the shift in an individual's personality when they are feeling stressed or disintegrated. Each type has two lines that connect it to other points on the Enneagram. Depending on the type of situation that the person is facing, they tend to adopt or embody the characteristics of a certain other type. Here are the directions of the lines that illustrate the stress embodiment: One shifts to Four, Four shifts to Two, Two moves to Eight, Eight moves to Five, five moves to Seven, and Seven moves to One. Within the triangle, Nine shifts to Six, Six shifts to Three, and Three shifts to Nine. When individuals are feeling safe and secure, and perceive themselves as healthy, there is the secure embodiment. The lines that illustrate the shift to a secure embodiment are such: One shifts to Seven, Seven moves to Five, Five moves to Eight, Eight shifts to Two, Two shifts to Four, and Four shift to One. IN the triangle, Nine moves to Three, Three shifts to Six, and Six shifts to Nine.

Wings of a personality certainly complicate things, but the geometry of the Enneagram is such that it holds a pattern and organization. There are many different ways to look at the Enneagram. It may make sense to consider it a cycle in itself, starting from the Type One, moving to the Type Two, and down along the line.

The Type Nine, the Peacemaker, is where the cycle restarts. The Wings for a personality inform and affect the way that the personality is expressed. The Perfectionist, while having a huge drive for perfections, will sometimes find the need to help people as a "perfect" endeavor. This would demonstrate the Type One taking on the characteristics of its wing on that side. The Performer will sometimes find that they want to "perform" as a helper. This would be the Performer's wing of Type Two impacting the Performer. Sometimes the Performer will have an artistic bent, and will take up cello or painting or writing. It's no coincidence that the Performer is situated next to the Romantic, who is desperately in love with all forms of art.

Chapter 6: Type Two– The Helper

People who have a Type Two personality are labeled as helpers because they are warm-hearted and empathetic. Their goal is to help people and serve others while sometimes neglecting their own needs.

Type Twos genuinely try their best to help others whenever they can, but they also love to be recognized as being helpful.

They feel sharing love and concern for others is the best way to live. Family and friendship are especially important to type Two personalities.

Type twos are understanding and compassionate. They have seemingly unlimited patience and are always willing to help out. A healthy Two will know how and when to let go of people in their life, while unhealthier type Twos have a hard time letting go and insist on being needed.

People are drawn to type Twos and many times take advantage of type Two's generosity.

They are well-meaning but sometimes their drive to help others becomes a need to be needed. They often have problems recognizing and admitting their own needs.

Their basic desire to feel loved leads to a central fear of being unwanted or unworthy of love.

Type Twos' development may be hindered by their tendency to become over-

involved in the lives of those around them.

Self-development requires visiting dark places in our subconscious – a place Type Twos avoid. They prefer to see themselves as completely positive and full of light.

The biggest obstacle for Type Twos (along with Threes and Fours centered around a common sense of shame) is facing their fear of being worthless to others. They feel they are nothing without their great acts of service.

Unhealthy Twos validate their self-worth by how much of themselves they sacrifice for others. They trade generosity and over-involvement as a means to obtain the love they secretly desire.

Type Twos with a One-wing may fall into the role of a servant. They direct their need to be needed to serving others, many times to a fault.

Type Twos with a Three-wing may serve the role of a host/hostess. They enjoy being able to bring people closer together.

Stress Point

When Type Twos are stressed, they may exhibit negative or unhealthy levels of development typically seen in Type Eight personalities.

These unhealthy traits include:

Vengeful

Murderous

Sociopathic

Callous

Hard-hearted

Antisocial

Totalitarianism

Feel invincible

Reckless

Dictatorial

Immoral

Violent

Confrontational

Threatening

Proud

Domineering

Self-sufficient

Security Point

During times of growth Type Twos may exhibit positive or healthy levels of development typically seen in Type Fours personalities.

These healthy traits include:

Creative

Inspired

Self-aware

Sensitive to others

Gentle

Tactful

Compassionate

Individualistic

Humane

Levels of Development

Healthy:

Level 1

Humble

Healthy level Twos are unselfish and altruistic. They have unconditional love to offer others. They consider it a privilege to be involved in the lives of others.

Level 2

Compassionate

Type Twos in this stage of development have sincere empathy for the feelings of others. They truly care about the needs of others. They are sincere, warm-hearted, thoughtful and forgiving towards others.

Level 3

Encouraging

They see the good in others. This level of development remembers to take care of their self as well as others. They are nurturing and generous in their giving – a truly loving person.

Average:

Level 4

People-pleasers

In an attempt to please the people around them, Twos may try to show off their loving nature and attempt to become too close to people.

Level 5

Overly intrusive

They develop a need to be needed. They try to meddle and control the lives of others in the name of love. They start to become codependent and self-sacrificial. They believe they can never do enough for others.

Level 6

Overbearing

They become a "martyr" for others. They may overrate their efforts for the benefit of others. They believe they are indispensable, other people need them. At times, they may be patronizing and presumptuous.

Unhealthy:

Level 7

Manipulative

Level 7 Type Two are self-serving. They tell people how much the other person "owes" them. They may abuse food or drugs to "stuff their feelings" and get sympathy from the people around them. They may make belittling remarks to undermine people. They are self-deceptive about how damaging their behavior and motives are.

Level 8

Coercive

This stage of Twos may become domineering. They feel they are entitled to repayment for all the service they gave to others.

Level 9

Victims

They rationalize their behavior by becoming victims. They are angry and resentful toward others. Many people in this stage resemble or become Hypochondriacs. They use health problems real, or imagined, to get attention.

Chapter 7: Physical Appearance

Did you know that your physical appearance could give others signs of your personality type? All those who belong to a specific Enneagram type tend to share certain physical similarities as well. In this section, you will learn about the general physical appearance of each of the Enneagram types.

Type One

The physical appearance of most of the Ones is such that it represents their inner dryness. Ones often tend to be thin and lean, at times to the extremes. Male Ones tend to prefer a beard or mustache. In some extreme cases, Ones can be obese too, but it is quite rare. They are usually tall, stand up straight, and use limited gestures. Ones tend to have an aura of being spare and rigid. Their smiles are often restrained but whenever they smile, it is always genuine. Ones like neatness and order, and the same shows in their physical appearance as well.

Type Two

Twos tend to opt for clothes that are conservative yet stylish. Neatness is very important for them. Twos are often elegant, poised, and like to add a little color to their outfit in a manner that is quietly distinctive – something like a colorful tie or an item of statement jewelry. In a social setting, Twos seem a little formal. Men and women with this Enneagram type like to be well groomed always.

Type Three

Threes like to look their fashionable best. Their clothes are always well chosen and reflect the current fashion trends. Threes are conscious of their weight, and they would never let themselves become obese. The clothes they opt for often express their calm and cheerful nature. Threes also like to look attractive and sexy.

Type Four

Fours like to present themselves to the world artfully and tastefully. Their idea of fashion often involves the combination of black with other cheerful colors. They usually have a medium build. Did you ever come across men and women dressed in outrageous costumes? Well, if you did, then it is highly likely that they were a Four or a Seven (more on that later).

Type Five

Fives are usually not too keen on their appearance. The best way to describe a five will be reasonable, ordinary, and nothing too bold. Most of the Fives tend to have glasses. Fives tend to carry a disheveled look. Fives with a strong Four wing tend to love interesting items of clothing. There is a strong chance that a person with messy hair and askew spectacles is a Type Five.

Type Six

Sixes have an innate desire to be likable and appealing. There are only two extremes that Sixes have - they can either be extremely attractive or scruffy and nothing in between. Sixes like to project that they are tough, even when they aren't. It is entirely unintentional that their body language comes across as being defensive or accusatory.

Type Seven

Sevens can be quite vain but their clothing options are usually gender-neutral. Sevens love color and they want to be noticed. They tend to lack the finesse that a Four has when it comes to fashion. So, the clothes that a Seven opts for are often loud and over the top. Aesthetics aren't something that Sevens can be bothered with.

Type Eight

Eights take a lot of care about their appearance. Slick and well dressed are the two common adjectives that perfectly describe an Eight. However, the way they dress depends on their mood and situations. For instance, when an Eight is happy and feels empowered, he looks quite elegant and dapper. However, if he isn't in a good mood, then it's the exact opposite. Eights mood dictates the way they present themselves. Most of them tend to have large features and a rough or rugged look.

Type Nine

Nines tend to be physically big. They are blessed with long and solid bones. Their movements are fluid and graceful when they are at ease. If a Nine is disturbed, he often comes across as being clumsy and uncoordinated. Their fashion choices are often tradition and are seldom loud or flashy. Nines don't crave for attention, and their sense of style represents the same.

Well, it isn't quite easy to identify someone's Enneagram type solely based on his or her looks. However, the points discussed in this chapter will come in handy to identify the person and their enneagram. Once you learn to identify Enneagram personalities, you will soon be able to find certain physical similarities among the same types.

Chapter 8: The Loyalist Subtypes

The three subtypes associated with the loyalist are warmth, intimidation, and duty. You can learn more about these subtypes and what they mean below.

Self-Preservation: Warmth

Loyalists have a tendency to be very anxious, which results in them feeling fearful and insecure. They become extremely cautious of most situations, including circumstantial and social. As a result of this tendency, the loyalist will often create a sense of security by building strong, reliable alliances and relationships with other people in their lives.

The loyalist is a truly warm-hearted and affectionate person, so the relationships they form on the basis of their warm nature is sincere and true. Sometimes, however, they will repress their anger and may be hesitant to share their true opinions, feelings, or beliefs with others to refrain from causing conflict. They prefer to be cautious and kind towards everyone so that they don't lose the people in their lives, rather than being honest and risking the conflict.

One-on-One: Intimidation

Another way of keeping themselves in a state of feeling secure instead of anxious and fearful is by being bold and intimidating toward others. The loyalist may be known to be excessively assertive over their opinions, beliefs, and feelings as a way to defend themselves and stay on the offense. They are typically quite reactive.

Rather than running away from fear, the loyalist with the intimidating subtype will run directly at it as an attempt to confront it and win every single time. They can be rebellious and even a daredevil with this subtype as a result of their need to feel strong and safe.

When a loyalist is living dominantly in the intimidation subtype, they may struggle to make connections with other people or have close friends as a result. This can result in them having greater doubts, feelings of vulnerability, and fears around relationships. This can be painful for the secretly sensitive intimidating loyalist.

Social: Duty

If a loyalist is dominant in the subtype of duty, they are known to be passionate about standing up for the underdog. When they see someone as weak or incapable of fully standing up for themselves, they will take it upon themselves to stand up for them. They may become highly passionate in charitable work or other activist-based activities.

Loyalists with the duty subtype typically like to follow rules and predetermined procedures and are often precise and very careful in their actions to ensure that they are doing things right. They feel a strong sense of duty for others and are typically operating from a highly rational state. These loyalists have a strong sense for justice and like to encourage others to bide by the rules as well. They are also great at making sure that everyone else knows what is expected of them.

Chapter 9: Creating Legendary Leadership

With The Enneagram

Many of you will know that I am passionate about how the Enneagram builds extraordinary awareness of itself as a way to turn your life and work in endless positive directions.

It is an extraordinarily dynamic and consequential personality profiling framework, which shows how your life orientation affects your happiness, success, efficiency, and perception by others. It shows you how you can move to your full potential and also how you can sabotage and retain yourself.

In my executive coaching (with people and teams), I currently use Enneagram to help them understand and maximize their individual style of leaders and that of their colleagues. Last November, with the New York Enneagram Institute, I completed an advanced course (Nine Domains) using the

Enneagram to build teams to their full potential.

Knowing how your particular Enneagram type builds your signature style and the potentials (and the pitfalls) of your individual approach and person is not only enlightening but also essential to create your own true way of leading your team and organization.

Here are some short examples of leadership opportunities and types of traps: type 1: the idealist or reformer+type 1 is truly visionary, idealist, enthusiastic about their personal leadership role, and their business mission. As such, their team will inspire new levels of success, commitment, and excitement.

Type 1s could be self-critical painful challenging, along with their high standards and idealism all of them self and they lead by others. That could be degrading and no productive, with Type 1s sometimes considered by direct report to colleagues to be too harsh and rigid taskmasters.

Type 2: The Helper or Carer + Type 2s lead with their hearts and inspire their team with emotional connectivity and empathy.

-Type 2s can become too emotional and particularly susceptible to derailment when personal or professional relationships collapse; Sometimes you can use emotional blackmail if you feel helpless, It directly undermines effective management.

Type 3: Achiever + Type 3s are enthusiastic about perfection, and many successful managers are of this type. Their commitment to success (sometimes almost at all costs) often guarantees excellent results and their team's accompanying commitment.

Three people are driven so that they do all they can to achieve "success" at all costs, leading to inauthentic leadership where three people burn themselves and their teams out and lose their relationships to priorities and values.

Type 4: Personal / Creative+Type 4 are often beautiful, charismatic, innovative, and motivated insightful thinkers. They can sometimes get rid of their own individual values and talents by encouraging their teams to succeed in the same manner if they feel not appreciated or if they feel they are not given adequate room for the use of their individual leadership style and abilities to shine. If that happens, they can be too individualistic, too dramatic, and intense, not team players.

Type 5: Thinker + Type 5 can be innovative, original, imaginative, intensely insightful leaders, capable of producing exceptional results in analytical and creative thinking.

-Type 5 can become disconnected members, lose the ability to communicate and inspire their group and find themselves excessively cold and distant.

Type 6: Type 6 loyalists are dedicated, hard work leaders who encourage their teams to be similar and often use humor as an effective strategy-if overwhelmed, 6 leaders are fooled by fear and negative actions, so focused on worst-case scenarios that they lose trust in their group, often leading to low morality and even panic.

Type 7: The Enthusiasts + Type 7 are enthusiastic, friendly, enjoyable leaders that can inspire their teams with the strength of their character and their energy. Seven managers can lose focus, get distracted, and lose their connection to their own emotional genuineness, and thus undermine their team and weaken collective focus and results.

Do you know your type of Enneagram? If so, why not find these points and how to improve your genuine leadership by working with your Enneagram style awareness?

The Enneagram Series of Personalities

For many centuries, the Enneagram has been present in various forms, most commonly referred to in this chapter as Enneagram of personalities, a combination of ancient wisdom and modern psychology. The term "Enneagram" means

"9 pointing stars" and refers to the conventional diagrammatic representation of the Enneagram.

Each of the 9 points refers to the way we look at the world in which we live: how we relate to it and how it concerns us. The nine ways to view the world are the techniques each of us has to respond to stressful or relaxed circumstances. In life, we tend to adopt one of these approaches rather than all others, and it affects the way we behave under different conditions.

The comparison of humans with a computer is a useful analogy to explain what the Enneagram is and what it does. A computer has the hardware, software, and memory; the operating system is central, without which the computer can't function.

Operating System: Windows Vista / Windows XP / Linux / MAC /

Other Hardware: hard drive, CD drive, Home computer, etc.

Software: CPU programs: a central processing unit that performs all calculations in the Memory of a computer.

The software RAM memory enables the computer to perform specific tasks and storage (RAM) along with the central processing unit.

Every few years, we update the computer operating system to take account of the latest developments in computer technology. Many of us now use the new Windows version. We know that if we try to use the most up-to-date technology with an outdated operating system, the program either does not work or does not. We know that the more programs we try to run concurrently, the more space we consume, the slower the computer; sometimes, even it crashes.

We also have the same setup in our human body:

Operating system: one of the nine Enneagram patterns

hardware: our body

software: the skills we have learned in life

memory: The brain

However, in contrast to the computer, most of us have not upgraded our operating system to take all the latest developments in life into account (our learning).

They seek to use the latest software while running an operating system that was first fully updated at the age of two and in the majority of cases no older than five. So we ask why these abilities are not supposed to produce the outcome (new software applied to an existing operating system). We also have a variety of unresolved life issues (open software files) that consumes greater and higher quantities of our CPU and memory; therefore, we get slower as life continues, and some of us also crashes (nerve breakdown).

This is a highly simplified comparison with the machine, but it makes the Enneagram's role in our lives very much apparent. Like on a computer, without our operating system, we can do very little.

Like in a computer, this operating system limits what we can do under the rules/limitations of the same operating system.

Why is all this benefiting you?

The Enneagram is the way out of this limiting circle. It gives us an understanding of the primary OS, which governs all of our actions and allows us to upgrade this system so that we can start working fully. How can we solve our lives ' problems if we don't know what causes this problem first?

In mapping, not only human behavior but also in sustainable personal development and transformation processes, the Enneagram model has been found to be very powerful. It has been used throughout its history to enable people to transcend their' operating system" self-imposed limitations.

The Personality of Business: Manage Your Style for Greater Success

Just as you are developing ways to get to work, eat lunch, and organize files, you are developing ways of thinking, perceiving, and energy. Consider, for example, a director whose habit of anticipating what might go wrong prevents him from taking the potential of new ideas completely into account. His colleagues view his impassioned criticism as pathological negativism and wonder why he can't get behind the group.

Or take a new department head whose habit of avoiding conflict prevents him from confronting poor performers and making changes to the workflow. Her employees are becoming impatient as she gathers more and more information while she begins to worry about her incapacity to prioritize and articulate a clear course of action.

Both examples show how the "reality" of any given situation is consistent with our preconceived ideas about how things are or should be. While hard ability gaps are fairly easy to identify and fill in, like knowing the balance sheet, it is often more difficult to define personal assumptions and values that can hinder our effectivity.

An Enneagram is a development tool that describes nine different personality types and how each information is filtered. It offers a practical method for understanding personality-based inclinations and how they influence the meaning that you assign to events and actions.

Each of the nine types of personalities can be considered as perceptive lenses. Every lens focuses on certain things (these are natural talents and strengths), distorting certain areas (these are blind spots). Your beliefs focus your attention on 'proof' that supports your ideas on how things should be.

The key psychological driving forces for each Enneagram category are as follows:

One person is motivated because of the need to do things in the right way and focus on mistakes Two people are motivated by a need to appreciate and concentrate on what others need Three people are motivated by a need to excel and focus on tasks and goals.

Persons of Category 1 are driven by a need to do things in the right direction and focus on errors

Type 2 people are motivated by a need to like themselves and focus on what other persons need

Type 3 persons are motivated by the need to excel and concentrate on tasks and goals. However, once you have become aware of restricting habits, new ways of thinking that have a more balanced perspective will replace them.

Here's a coaching customer example. This director worked very long hours and achieved very little on tasks. It became apparent after several coaching sessions (e.g., a taped interview) that this director was Enneagram Type Two. When she learned more about Twos's interpretation and processing of data, she saw that she never retreated when she asked for additional tasks and got resentful of all her tasks.

One of the coaching activities of this director was to write down each time she said yes to additional tasks over two weeks. There have been some trends. She needed her boss ' support and also wanted to protect him from repercussions if departmental goals were not achieved. She was also concerned that she would not like her colleagues if she said no to their demands.

This boss has started clearing her plate of non-critical work for the next few months and delegating more to her assistants. She learned to discriminate against what she said yes and took some risks to say no. Since interpersonal skills are strong, she has become (instead of taking responsibility for) a mentor for colleagues and has found that giving employees more independence frees up her time to focus on genuine priorities.

In combination with coaching as well as other development activities, the

Enneagram is particularly effective in helping people learn new skills, increase their confidence, and become better leaders. The insights into motivation allow individuals to shift their perception to a fundamental level and see how they can get away from themselves. The outcomes are a better use of resources, greater resourcefulness in meeting problems, and a wider view of what is possible.

Chapter 10: The Helper

You have a purpose to bond with others and help them. You love to make a difference in the lives of the people you meet and intuitively know what other people sometimes need, better than they know themselves.

Watch out for the times you put other people's needs before your own. There will be times when you need to do this, but this cannot become a regular habit. Otherwise, you will burn yourself out. Remember your relationship with yourself is just as important as the relationship you have with your family, friends, colleagues, and even strangers.

At your best, you are a gift to the world offering generous hospitality wherever you go. The gift is that you provide it without any expectations. It feels good to help when you can.

Helpers want to help the world and its mother. They tend to take on everyone's problems as they believe that they can fix them. Their primary motivation is pride - everyone, they tend to think, needs help.

Their positive qualities are that they are extremely kind and helpful to their fellow beings. They make wonderful supporters and righthand people as they essentially enjoy being the providers of help. The welfare of the individual is the most important thing.

The giver personality type does not, by and large, tend to make a good leader. They generally do not like goals and are not primarily task orientated. They can allow themselves to become too emotionally involved which can often lead to negative feelings, such as the impression of being used. These negative feelings can sometimes cause a lack of objectivity and they can easily lose sight of their role.

"If you're helping someone and expecting something in return, you're doing business not kindness" - Anonymous

People of this personality type essentially feel that they are worthy insofar as they are helpful to others. Love is their highest ideal. Selflessness is their duty. Giving to others is their reason for being. Involved, socially aware, usually extroverted, Twos are the type of people who remember everyone's birthday and who go the extra mile to help out a co-worker, spouse or friend in need.

Twos are warm, emotional people who care a great deal about their personal relationships, devote an enormous amount of energy to them, and who expect to be appreciated for their efforts. They are practical people who thrive in the helping professions and who know how to make a home comfortable and inviting. Helping others makes Twos feel good about themselves; being needed makes them feel important; being selfless, makes Twos feel virtuous. Much of a Two's self-image revolves around these issues, and any threat to that selfimage is scarcely tolerated. Twos are thoroughly convinced of their selflessness, and it is true that they are frequently genuinely helpful and concerned about others. It is equally true, however, that Twos require appreciation; they need to be needed. Their love is not entirely without ulterior motive.

Twos often develop a sense of entitlement when it comes to the people closest to them. Because they have extended themselves for others, they begin to feel that gratitude is owed to them. They can become intrusive and demanding if their often unacknowledged emotional needs go unmet. They can be bossy and manipulative, feeling entirely justified in being so, because they "have earned the right" and their intentions are good. The darkest side of the type Two fixation appears when the Two begins to feel that they will never receive the love they deserve for all of their efforts. Under such circumstances, they can become hysterical, irrational and even abusive.

Because Twos are generally helping others meet their needs, they can forget to take care of their own. This can lead to physical burnout, emotional exhaustion and emotional volatility. Twos need to learn that they can only be of true service to others if they are healthy, balanced and centered in themselves.

Twos can mistype themselves if they are not in an obvious helper role in their professional lives; they might not recognize the extent of their involvement in assisting others. This is especially true for male Twos, who have not received the same social rewards for helping as female Twos receive. Male Twos frequently mistype as Ones or Threes, the wings of type Two. Females, of all types, are bound to recognize some of the dynamics of type two in their personalities; as such qualities have been socially reinforced. Female Nines, for instance, are especially prone to mistyping as Twos, particularly if they are the mothers of small children. But Nines are self-effacing and humble; Twos are proud and have a strong sense of their own worth.

A bit like emotional sponges, Twos have to be very careful what they absorb from the people around them. Getting angry or setting personal boundaries can be very hard to do, although they may have emotional outbursts to relieve the pressure. While being a special person or earning the approval of others has its advantages, it doesn't substitute for being loved for oneself.

Strengths: Caring, popular, communicator

Problems: Privileged, naive, dependent

Speaking style: Being nice and sympathetic, giving advice, sometimes militant for the cause

Lower emotional habit: Pride about being special, important, or indispensable in relationship. Or poor self-esteem when approval is not forthcoming

Higher emotion: Humility, which is being able to know and hold onto the experience of self-worth without either self-inflation or excessive self-judgment

Archetypal challenge: To find oneself in relationship, balancing dependency and autonomy

Psychological defenses: Twos use the defense mechanism of repression to avoid their own needs and feelings and to maintain the self-image of being "helpful." (Repression is putting one's unacceptable feelings out of awareness and converting them into a more acceptable form of emotional energy).

Somatic patterns: As feeling types, Twos experience a buildup of energy, and sometimes tension, around their chest and diaphragm. Although full of energy in their upper bodies, it's hard for them to sense their lower bodies and stay grounded. They tend to discharge their anxiety thru talking and emoting. It's easy for them to "somatize" or convert hidden/repressed feelings into physical symptoms.

Two, as this personality type is called, is everyone's dream friend. They exist to give, and they place a high value on their relationships. They are helpful to a fault, and will readily volunteer their services if you need it. Nothing is too bothersome for two. Your needs come first – that's how selfless they can be.

They remember everyone's birthday and anniversaries. They'll do your reports for you. They'll babysit your kids, and even stay and take care of you when you're sick. It's in their nature to give and put the needs of other people above their own.

Is Two, the Mother Teresa type? Are they saints? Do they give for the sake of giving, and ask for nothing in return? Unfortunately... no.

Don't misunderstand. Twos are usually genuinely happy when they serve others. They totally believe in their selflessness and their whole self-image revolves around it. They thrive as nurses, caregivers, doctors, homemakers, and in any profession that helps someone. They spend a lot of their time and efforts in their relationships with people, they sacrifice their own needs and desires for others... but they expect to be appreciated in return. Two's loving has an ulterior motive. They need to be needed to feel worthy. Their sense of worth is based on how helpful they are to someone.

In the act of helping others, they feel good about themselves. They feel important when somebody needs them. Selflessness makes two feel virtuous. These are the issues that get satisfied by the acts of helping and giving. It's unacceptable when these needs are not being met.

In the best light, Twos are popular, expressive, friendly, welcoming, and quick to lend a helping hand. They believe they know what's best for others and they take pride in being able jump in and assist people in some way.

Twos find it hard to say no, to anyone. They can't risk being unworthy of love.

They will adapt and change what they need to, to earn approval. They have no concept of personal boundaries. They are so wrapped up in other people that they can't tune in to their own feelings.

It's not unnatural to see two going through an emotional outburst to get some relief. It's hard to repress your own needs to avoid looking needy, and maintain a capable and helpful image. This repression can lead to burnout, resentment, and emotional exhaustion. You can't give others water if your own well is dry.

On the darker side, Twos have a tendency to develop a sense of entitlement. Since they've given so much to others, they demand gratitude. If this need is not satisfied, they can be demanding and intrusive, even manipulative. Like the psychos that you see in movies. They feel justified in their actions since they have earned the right. After all, haven't they done so much already?

Once they realize that they will never get the love and appreciation they deserve, even after all their efforts that are when two can come undone. They can become irrational, hysterical, and physically abusive.

You can turn your tendency to seek approval from others and your tendency to crave attention into the more positive attributes of compassion and focus on other human beings. This will help you to build long lasting friendships that help meet your underlying motivation to feel needed in a much more positive way

Chapter 11: Difference Between The Types Of Enneagram

This chapter will do justice to the difference between each personality type or group and explains the difference between them. You are expected to pay attention to the weaknesses and strengths of each type. It will also do you a lot of good if you can understand how those personalities make up for each other in one way or the other.

Let us take a keen look at each of the personalities. We will also look at how they can influence your relationship positively.

Group 1: The Reformers

Reformers are the conscientious and ethical fellows, with a strong sense of what is right and what is wrong and should be avoided. They seek perfection always and feel a dutiful responsibility to change and improve things for the better. They are often highly detailed, organized, and love to see things done orderly, quality, and diligence to teams are what they continuously seek.

Reformers can be very critical of those around them as they always want the best from them. Their perfection-seeking behavior, which is sometimes sickening, can come at the cost of delivering value early or personal burn out, going the extra mile, working extremely long hours to get the job done to their own high standards and it can also come at the sacrifice of personal joy.

At their very best, they are so wise, discerning, and a noble set of people. So, in a relationship, they are expected to always push their teammates, partners, colleagues, spouse and be the constant leader. A reformer should help to reform and make a relationship work.

Group 2: The Helpers

Helpers, out of all other groups, are the most relationship-focused group. They are so empathetic, supportive, and sincere to their partners. Their relationship focus and commitments help build healthy cultures but can eventually become overly focused on the happiness and support of others at their detriment and at the same time they can lose focus of the need for productivity, results and needed outcomes. They often take on supporting, directing, coaching, schooling, modeling or mentoring roles in a different relationship be it love or work relationship, which then eventually provide the much-needed individual growth for those in the organization or relationship which they are trying to assist and help grow. Their primary focus on others can make them burn themselves out, at which point they can eventually become stressed and totally worn out. At their very best, they are so altruistic and have unconditional love for others in the relationship.

Group 3: The Achievers

Achievers are the self-assured types, and they are very charismatic as an enneagram group. They are so ambitious, goal-oriented, outcome-focused, and highly driven to achieve success and have the needed results. They always bring a focus on goals and productivity to teams and organizations, which can sometimes make them detach themselves from what they see as unproductive cases and events, which include some team building programs.

Achievers often rise astronomically to leadership roles and can easily balance out over perfectionist technical cultures in an unprecedented way. They are also known as chameleons because they can adapt to situations. They also give the capacity to read situations, analyze it and can quickly change or overhaul or blend their style to achieve the required success which they go extra miles to achieve. Achievers sometimes over associate with status and roles, in their need to feel valuable. At their very best, they are known to be self-accepting and authentic role models for others who look up to them.

Group 4: The Individualists

The individualists are self-aware, sensitive, and highly reserved to the extent that they can be so calm in the face of adversity. They are often innovative types drawn to novel ideas and creative things. Through the arts of creating new products either as designers, originators, or developers who get the product to the people who need to see. They love to be deeply involved in creating meaning for things and they mostly value work tied to a more significant meaning, challenge, purpose, and cause. Motivation can be the main challenge for an individualist, as they often try to avoid whatever they see as highly mundane, ordinary activities or inconsequential practice that may be too detailed in nature. They are often idea propagators and innovative pioneers. They love to connect seemingly disjointed topics in new yet inventive ways and manners. Under high stress, individualists can become too moody and very difficult to manage by a partner, manager or their spouse. They sometimes seek special attention and treatment from their colleagues and partners. When you know all this, it will become effortless for you to manage your partners.

At their very best, individualists are always inspired by the things around them and can serve as a model for their partners. They are also highly creative and can quickly get involved in critical thinking. More so, they find it easy to renew themselves, transform their experience into tangible yet useful things. At their lowest, they can be insipid. It is now expected of their partners, team members to use the strength of this group for the betterment of their relationship. If you are dealing with an individualist, you must understand that he is a dreamer and you must be ready to operate at the poetic realm and ideal world to flow with him. Knowing the strengths and weaknesses of this group will go a long way in determining whether your relationship will survive or not.

Group 5: The Investigators

Investigators are vigilant, critically insightful, curious and inquisitive. They are highly motivated by intellectual capability and demonstrate ability and competency in anything that is being done by them. They like to present a very sound yet logical personality that survives on mental rigors and in-depth knowledge. They are also known to be innovative, inventive, trendsetters as they always research things that seem obscure. They can easily become preoccupied with their personal thoughts, ideas and some imaginary constructs which other groups might find tasking and esoteric.

The relationship challenges for the investigators is to move from the enjoyments that are associated with relationship and problem-solving phase to that of growing, nurturing and making their relationship work and last. At their very best, they are visionary, pioneers, who love to share their lofty ideas, knowledge, and insights with their partners. For a relationship to work out for this group, they must try to be less critical of others as they sometimes get on the nerves of their colleague and partners through too much questioning,

Type 6: The Loyalist

Loyalists are reliable, committed, trustworthy, and excellent troubleshooters set of people. They are usually visionaries and are able to foresee problems and challenges and bring their partners, spouse, and staff together to find a solution to the envisaged or encountered problem. However, loyalists can get wrapped up in what is known as "cycles of analysis paralysis" which often makes them too anxious and highly stressed when they spot a problem.

Loyalists focus on standard operations, culture, religion, ethics, and they love being loyal to their partners and team, tribe, society, community, or organization. This helps to establish a collaborative way of working and finding solution to problems. They sometimes seek guidance from a persuasive authority, mentors, sources, leaders, established channels or superior. They love to use the advice that is given to them by their mentors as a guiding light through their self-doubt, self-pity, and relationship. At their very best, they are internally stable and have peace of mind. They are courageous, brave and loyal to the game, culture and their relationship. Being in contact with loyalists could be the best thing as this helps their partner, spouse or colleague to have a smooth sailing since there is a dependable team member in the team who can go out of his way to get solution to any issue being confronted by the whole team. It is expected of you, being a loyalist, to always carry your partner along in your relationship. However, if you want your relationship to really grow, you should not expect much from your partner because they are wired in different ways. If you are in a relationship with a loyalist, always strive hard not to betray their trust as that may prove very fatal. They can be mean when taken for a ride.

Group 7: The Enthusiasts

Enthusiasts, as can be deduced from their name, are so jovial, enthusiastic, spontaneous, and highly optimistic. Their fun-loving and vibrant nature brings positive energy into their environments at all time, and they are sometimes the very ones championing new innovations, ideas and that make them able to always see the big picture. Their energy can easily and quickly become scattered, shattered under little stress, which can make them falter when they know that they would have to struggle to complete the plethora of activities they have laid out or initiated.

They are mostly practical and quick in their thinking. They love to focus on being busy and moving at all times. At their very best, they are profoundly rooted and grounded which makes them focus on achieving meaningful goals and realizing their missions. They are so appreciative and are easily satisfied with whatever they have and whatever they can achieve. Being in a relationship with an enthusiast means that their partner must charge them to go far or the relationship will not work out.

Partners must always be in sync with them for them to achieve greater things and their partners must not be dull or moody if they are to achieve good things together or go extra miles.

Group 8: The Challengers

Challengers are so confident, assertive, opinionated, protective, and proactive, straight-talking, and blunt set of people. They are so decisive in actions, but can also be too demanding and highly controlling in their approach. Challengers always want to control their environments and love to shy away from any personal injury and vulnerability that may make them look weak. Their characteristics sometimes help them rise in career or quickly get a relationship, or make them reach zenith of their career and get commiserating leadership roles. Also, their features also make it possible for them to find it challenging to maintain momentum or lead. They often struggle to lead at the level, where vulnerability and useful engagement of other members play a very significant part in the success or otherwise of a relationship or organization.

Challengers are clannish, and they are extremely protective of their tribe, their people or race or team members and can become highly a savage whenever they believe that they or their group, clan, tribe, partner or race is being attacked or cheated by other people outside their group. At their very best, challenger's version changes, they do not shirk from what they see as their responsibilities to lead others. And they also stand in the frontline of the battle to improve the welfare of their clan, partners or team members. Being in a relationship with this type can be so good as it shows that you have a reliable someone whom you know will always have your back. As a challenger, you must find someone who is trustworthy before you can establish a relationship with them.

Group 9: The Peacemakers

Peacemakers are such a calm, stable, peaceful, trusting and meek, humble set of people. By their very nature, they love to be in a serene environment. They often agree with other people's views and abide by their points to keep the environment peaceful and calm. Most times, they lose sight of their own preferences, beliefs, and views in the process of pleasing other people. They see harmony in the world and use this to facilitate peace wherever they find themselves. Like the loyalists mentioned above, peacemakers also help create peace and positive movements that seek the good of every member of the society. They sometimes work to balance things out between two warring factions. They serve as the balance for the challengers as they help to mop out the ripple effect of what are usually caused by the challengers' personalities and behaviors.

Peacemakers can constantly struggle to motivate themselves and can be deemed as stubborn or aggressively inactive to other groups.

At their very best, they are all-embracing and see no colors, religions, tribes, or dissimilarities, what they always look out for is what binds people together and not what divides them. It is in their nature to bring different types of people together and heal conflict where it is appropriate and necessary. Being in a relationship with peacemakers is the best thing to happen to any other enneagram of personality from group one to group eight. This is because they will serve as a balance for others and make them become a better version of them. They also do not hold grudges as they hate conflict or anything that can bring fight, war or disharmony. However, to improve your relationship, you have to push peacemakers to achieve their true potentials. Therefore, you must be ready to help them grow and advise them on what they should do and what they should not if they are to rise above their current level.

Chapter 12: Type Two – The Helper

Type Two in a word

Twos are sympathetic, earnest, and pleasant. They are inviting, liberal, and generous, yet can likewise be wistful, complimenting, and human satisfying. They are benevolent and headed to be near others, however can slip into getting things done for others so as to be required. They commonly have issues with possessiveness and with recognizing their own needs.

At their Best: unselfish and benevolent, they have unrestricted love for other people.

Fundamental Fear: Of being undesirable, dishonorable of being adored

Fundamental Desire: To feel adored

Enneagram Two with a One-Wing: "Hireling"

Enneagram Two with a Three-Wing: "The Host/Hostess"

Key Motivations: Want to be adored, to express their affections for other people, to be required and acknowledged, to get others to react to them, to vindicate their cases about themselves.

The Meaning of the Arrows (in a word)

While moving in their Direction of Disintegration (stress), destitute Twos all of a sudden become forceful and commanding at Eight. In any case, while moving in their Direction of Integration (development), prideful, self-misleading Twos become increasingly self-supporting and sincerely mindful, as sound Fours. Become familiar with the bolts.

Models: Paramahansa Yogananda, Pope John XXIII, Guru Ammaji ("The Hugging Saint"), Byron Katie, Bishop Desmond Tutu, Eleanor Roosevelt, Nancy Reagan, Monica Lewinsky, Ann Landers, Mary Kay Ash (Mary Kay Cosmetics), Leo Buscaglia, Richard Simmons, Luciano Pavarotti, John Denver, Lionel Richie, Stevie Wonder, Barry Manilow, Dolly Parton, Josh Groban, Music of Journey, Bobby McFerrin, Kenny

G, Paula Abdul, Priscilla Presley, Elizabeth Taylor, Danny Thomas, Martin Sheen, Jennifer Tilly, Danny Glover, Richard Thomas "John Boy Walton," Juliette Binoche, Arsenio Hall, Timothy Treadwell "Grizzly Man," "Melanie Hamilton Wilkes" (Gone with the Wind), "Eve Harrington" (All About Eve), "Dr. McCoy"

Enneagram Type 2 - The Helper

Type 1 - Perfectionist

Type 2 - Helper

Type 3 - Performer

Type 4 - Romantic

Type 5 - Observer

Type 6 - Loyal Skeptic

Type 7 - Epicure

Type 8 - Protector

Type 9 - Mediator

Twos are an inclination put together type with a concentration with respect to relationship. They exceed expectations at making associations and relating to the requirements and sentiments of others.

They are typically great at supporting others and drawing out their latent capacity. Nonetheless, turning their consideration toward themselves and recognizing what they themselves need is significantly more troublesome. They need to be acknowledged and loved by others, and they will adjust or change themselves to procure this endorsement.

Somewhat like enthusiastic wipes, Twos must be exceptionally cautious what they ingest from the individuals around them. Blowing up or defining individual limits can be difficult to do, in spite of the fact that they may have enthusiastic upheavals to mitigate the weight. While being a unique individual or procuring the endorsement of others has its focal points, it doesn't fill in for being cherished for oneself.

Qualities: Caring, well known, communicator

Issues: Privileged, innocent, subordinate

Talking style: Being pleasant and thoughtful, offering guidance, at times aggressor for the reason

Lower enthusiastic propensity: Pride about being unique, significant, or crucial in relationship. Or then again poor confidence when endorsement isn't expected

Higher feeling: Humility, which is having the option to know and clutch the experience of self-esteem without either self-swelling or over the top self-judgment

Model test: To wind up in relationship, adjusting reliance and self-sufficiency

Mental protections: Twos utilize the guard component of restraint to keep away from their own needs and sentiments and to keep up the mental self-view of being "useful." (Repression is putting one's unsatisfactory emotions out of mindfulness and changing over them into a progressively worthy type of passionate vitality).

Substantial examples: As feeling types, Twos experience a development of vitality, and at times strain, around their chest and stomach. Albeit brimming with vitality in their chest areas, it's difficult for them to detect their lower bodies and stay grounded. They will in general release their tension through talking and emoting. It's simple for them to "somatize" or convert covered up/curbed sentiments into physical indications.

Type Two Overview

We have named character type Two The Helper since individuals of this sort are either the most really accommodating to others or, when they are less solid, they are simply the most exceptionally put resources into seeing as supportive. Being liberal and making a special effort for others makes Twos feel that theirs is the most extravagant, most significant approach to live. The adoration and concern they feel—and the veritable great they do—makes them feel good inside and make them feel beneficial. Twos are generally inspired by what they feel to be the "incredibly great" things throughout everyday life—love, closeness, sharing, family, and fellowship.

Louise is a pastor who shares the delight she finds in being a Two.

"I can't envision being another sort and I would not have any desire to be another sort. I like being associated with people groups' lives. I like inclination caring, mindful, sustaining. I like cooking and homemaking. I like having the certainty that anybody can disclose to me anything about themselves and I will have the option to cherish them.... I am extremely pleased with myself and love myself for having the option to be with individuals where they are. I truly can, and do, love individuals, pets, and things. Furthermore, I am an incredible cook!"

At the point when Twos are solid and in balance, they truly are adoring, useful, liberal, and thoughtful. Individuals are attracted to them like honey bees to nectar. Solid Twos warm others in the sparkle of their souls. They breathe life into others with their gratefulness and consideration, helping individuals to see positive characteristics in themselves that they had not recently perceived. To put it plainly, sound Twos are the epitome of "the great parent" that everybody wishes they had: somebody who considers them to be they are, comprehends them with gigantic empathy, helps and supports with unending persistence, and is continually ready to assist—while knowing absolutely how and when to give up. Sound Twos open our hearts in light of the fact that theirs are as of now so open and they show us the best approach to be all the more profoundly and luxuriously human.

Louise proceeds:

"The entirety of my occupations spun around helping individuals. I was an educator who needed to be touchy to kids and assist them with getting off to a decent start. I was strict instruction chief in various areas. I imagined that if individuals found out about the profound life, they'd be more joyful... The most significant piece of my life is my otherworldly life. I was in a strict network for a long time. I wedded a previous cleric, and we both have our otherworldliness as a mind-blowing premise together."

Be that as it may, Twos' inward improvement might be constrained by their "shadow side"— pride, self-trickery, the inclination to become over-engaged with the lives of others, and the propensity to control others to get their own enthusiastic needs met. Transformational work involves going into dim places in ourselves, and this particularly runs contrary to the natural order of things of the Two's character structure, which wants to see itself in just the best, gleaming terms.

Maybe the greatest snag confronting Twos, Threes, and Fours in their inward work is confronting their fundamental Center dread of uselessness. Underneath the surface, each of the three sorts dread that they are without esteem in themselves, thus they should be or accomplish something remarkable so as to win love and acknowledgment from others. In the normal to undesirable

Levels, Twos present a bogus picture of being totally liberal and unselfish and of not needing any sort of pay-off for themselves, when truth be told, they can have tremendous desires and unacknowledged passionate needs.

Normal to unfortunate Twos look for approval of their value by complying with their superego's requests to forfeit themselves for other people. They accept they should consistently put others first and be adoring and unselfish on the off chance that they need to get love. The issue is that "putting others first" irritates Twos and angry emotions they make a solid effort to subdue or deny. By and by, they in the long run eject in different ways, upsetting Twos' connections and uncovering the inauthenticity of a significant number of the normal to undesirable Two's cases about themselves and the profundity of their "adoration."

Two, as this character type is called, is everybody's fantasy companion. They exist to give, and they place a high incentive on their connections. They are useful to say the least, and will promptly volunteer their administrations on the off chance that you need it. Nothing is unreasonably annoying for Two. Your needs started things out – that is the way sacrificial they can be.

They recollect everybody's birthday and commemorations. They'll do your reports for you. They'll mind kids, and even remain and deal with you when you're wiped out. It's in their tendency to give and put the necessities of others over their own.

Is Two, the Mother Teresa type? It is safe to say that they are holy people? Do they give for giving, and request nothing consequently? Shockingly... no.

Try not to misjudge. Twos are normally really cheerful when they serve others. They absolutely trust in their benevolence and their entire mental self-view rotates around it. They flourish as medical attendants, guardians, specialists, homemakers, and in any calling that helps somebody. They invest a great deal of their energy and endeavors in their associations with individuals, they penance their own needs and wants for other people… yet they hope to be acknowledged in kind. Two's cherishing has an ulterior thought process. They should be expected to feel commendable. Their feeling of worth depends on the fact that they are so useful to somebody.

In the demonstration of helping other people, they like themselves. They feel significant when someone needs them. Benevolence makes Two feel temperate. These are the issues that get fulfilled by the demonstrations of aiding and giving. It's unsuitable when these requirements are not being met.

In the best light, Twos are well known, expressive, inviting, and snappy to loan some assistance. They accept they recognize what's best for other people, and they invest wholeheartedly in being capable bounce in and help individuals somehow or another.

Twos think that it's difficult to state no, to anybody. They can't chance being dishonorable of affection. They will adjust and change what they have to, to acquire endorsement. They have no understanding of individual limits. They are so enveloped with others that they can't check out their own sentiments.

It's not unnatural to see Twos experiencing a passionate upheaval to get some help. It's difficult to quell your own needs to abstain from looking destitute, and keep up a competent and accommodating picture. This suppression can prompt burnout, hatred, and enthusiastic fatigue. You can't give others water if your own well is dry.

On the darker side, Twos tend to build up a feeling of qualification. Since they've given such a great amount to other people, they request appreciation. In the event that this need isn't fulfilled, they can be requesting and meddlesome, even manipulative. Like the psychos that you find in motion pictures. They feel supported in their activities since they have earned the right. All things considered, haven't they accomplished such a great deal as of now?

When they understand that they will never get the affection and thankfulness they merit, considerably after the entirety of their endeavors, that is when Two can come unraveled. They can get silly, insane, and physically damaging.

The most effective method to Get Along with a Two

A grateful word for Two, can go far.

Give affirmation that you esteem them regardless of whether they don't do anything for you.

Check out them for a change. They have requirements and emotions as well. (Despite the fact that they'd most likely move the consideration back to you.)

Be delicate when you scrutinize. Twos are extremely delicate.

Reveal to them they're extraordinary, and accomplish something decent for them from time to time.

On the off chance that they're very nearly a passionate upheaval, recognize their hatred and disappointment.

In spite of the fact that the Love of Two has a value, it's a little cost to pay for what this character type is eager to give.

Type Two – The Helper

The Enneagram Type Two character – the Helper – centers around connections and picking up endorsement. They present themselves as cheery, vigorous, and well disposed. They invest heavily in their capacity to "read" individuals and adjust their practices to suit the temperaments, inclinations, and requirements of others. They help individuals see what's sure about themselves, the individuals around them, and their surroundings.

Solid Twos are outstanding partners, companions, and relatives who put forth an admirable attempt to express their fondness and offer help. They are incredible audience members who revel in others' delights and tap profound wells of sympathy in the midst of distress or difficulty. Their inspiration can be irresistible. Should life bargain you lemons, they'll assist you with liking making lemonade.

While Twos plainly discover satisfaction in taking care of others' needs, their liberality for the most part conveys a desire for equal consideration. Some enneagram instructors catch this reasonableness by naming Type Twos Connectors. This classification causes to notice the way that Twos need their demonstrations of administration to fabricate ties that dilemma. You may state that they provide for get.

At the point when subject to the impact of the neighboring One, Healthy Twos become the Servant. Their drive to soothe enduring discovers friendship with a reality of direction toward powerful activity. They are frequently attracted to educating, open assistance, service, and mending callings. While they'll lead the charge should the need emerge, they're very substance to work in the background.

Whenever you're asked what your "type" is, it's very conceivable what your questioner is extremely after is which Enneagram Type you are. In spite of the fact that the historical backdrop of the Enneagram of Personality model is somewhat obfuscated, with some guaranteeing its sources date right back to fourth century Greece, the test as we as of now realize it met up during the 1950's under the bearing of a Bolivian analyst — and it's just picking up prominence today. That analyst recognized nine diverse Enneagram Types, and, given that you've arrived on a page about Type 2, "The Helper," we're speculating this particular kind is one you're interested to get familiar with.

What is the Enneagram Type 2 character?

Compassionate, true, and giving, Type 2 inside the Enneagram is known as "The Helper" which is as it should be. They need what is best for other people, are viewed as thoughtful and benevolent people, and are fit for giving an unlimited sort of affection. On the clouded side, this sort is frequently powerless to organizing others to the point of acting naturally yielding, as they neglect to recognize their own needs and limits. They can likewise tend to be somewhat possessive; given the measure of vitality they fill helping other people, it's maybe expected they would battle with the inclination they aren't as similarly organized. By the day's end, their most driving motivation is to be cherished. While moving toward pressure, this sort can all of a sudden become forceful and ruling; while pushing toward a "Course of Integration" (or development), be that as it may, Twos become all the more sincerely mindful and can expand their feeling of supporting internal, rather than just outward.

Type 2 are enormous hearted, merciful, sustaining, charitable and illustrative. They are sentiments-based individuals who can't envision a world where they aren't giving their vitality to helping other people. This people group driven sort is generally worried about what they see to be the signs of a well-lived: love, family, kinship, and enthusiastic closeness with others. In view of their constructive, productive, we-can-fix-this nearness, individuals will in general run to Twos like flies to nectar.

These persons are hearted, lenient, supporting, beneficent and illustrative. They are conclusion-based people who can't imagine an existence where they aren't giving their essentialness to helping others. This social order driven sort is commonly stressed over what they see to be the indications of a well-lived: love, family, connection, and excited closeness with others. In perspective on their valuable, profitable, we-can-fix-this proximity, people will when all is said in done race to Twos like flies to nectar.

Type Two—Levels of Development

Solid Levels

Level 1 (At Their Best): Become profoundly unselfish, humble, and philanthropic: giving unequivocal love to self as well as other people. Feel it is a benefit to be in the lives of others.

Level 2: Empathetic, merciful, feeling for other people. Thinking and worried about their needs. Attentive, caring, excusing and true.

Level 3: Encouraging and thankful, ready to see the positive qualities in others. Administration is significant, however deals with self as well: they are supporting, liberal, and giving—a genuinely cherishing individual.

Normal Levels

Level 4: Want to be nearer to other people, so start "individualsatisfying," getting excessively well disposed, sincerely decisive, and loaded with "honest goals" about everything. Give tempting consideration: endorsement, "strokes," sweet talk. Love is their preeminent worth, and they talk about it always.

Level 5: Become excessively private and nosy: they should be required, so they drift, interfere, and control for the sake of adoration. Need others to rely upon them:

give, however anticipate an arrival: send twofold messages. Wrapping and possessive: the mutually dependent, self-conciliatory individual who can't do what's necessary for other people—destroying themselves for everybody, making requirements for themselves to satisfy.

Level 6: Increasingly gaudy and smug, feel they are vital, in spite of the fact that they misrepresent their endeavors for others' sake. Neurosis, turning into a "saint" for other people. Tyrannical, belittling, pompous.

Undesirable Levels

Level 7: Can be manipulative and self-serving, imparting blame by telling others the amount they owe them and cause them to endure. Misuse nourishment and prescription to "stuff emotions" and get compassion. Undermine individuals, making putting down, defaming comments. Incredibly self-tricky about their intentions and how forceful and additionally egotistical their conduct is.

Level 8: Domineering and coercive: feel qualified to get anything they need from others: the reimbursement of old obligations, cash, sexual favors.

Level 9: Able to pardon and excuse what they do since they feel manhandled and exploited by others and are sharply angry and furious. Somatization of their hostilities brings about interminable medical issues as they vindicate themselves by "self-destructing" and troubling others. For the most part compares to the Histrionic Personality Disorder and Factitious Disorder.

Chapter 13: The Enneagram Personality

Type 5 - The Observer

This personality type is also called the Investigator. This person has a need to understand or to know and is supremely focused on gaining information and knowledge. This person loves to sit on the sidelines and observe from a distance before becoming engaged in new situations, new activities, and new people. They do this because they fear being viewed as incompetent, being unprepared, or being emotionally depleted by disengagement.

What Makes The Observer a Great Personality

THE OBSERVER IS ALERT AND INSIGHTFUL. This personality type wants to know why things work the way they do. This person yearns to possess knowledge and to understand their environment. This insight will allow them to defend themselves from threats from that environment. This personality type is always searching, asking questions, and delving deeper into subjects like the cosmos, the animal kingdom, and the microscopic world. This person does not just accept the opinion of other people but instead conducts their own investigations. They are so mentally grounded, Observers tend to be very intelligent thoughtful on a well-read. As a result, they are often expressed in the areas that capture their interest with many of them being scientifically oriented.

THE OBSERVER IS OFTEN AN EXPERT IN HIS OR HER CHOSEN FIELD. Observers are often relentless in their pursuit of knowledge and this allows them to easily master many subject areas and interests.

THE OBSERVER IS INDEPENDENT AND INNOVATIVE. This personality type does not depend on external validation and thus is very independent in their thinking and the way they live their life. These people are also visionaries because of the broad understanding they have of the world and the way it works.

THE OBSERVER IS UNMANIPULATIVE. Types 5s often come into relationships without agendas and are often simply fascinated by a person, hence their interest in forming a relationship.

The Deadly Sins of the Observer

THE OBSERVER FEARS BEING USELESS AND INCAPABLE. This person is the epiphany of thinking before acting. Behind their competency is a well of insecurity that stems from being viewed as helpless by other people.

THE OBSERVER ISOLATES HIS OR HERSELF. This person feels most comfortable in the realm of thought because they do not feel secure in their ability to handle life. Therefore, they tend to withdraw to the safety of the mind where they can mentally prepare to deal with other people, situations, and experiences. Type 5s are also reluctant to ask for help from others even though these people will be very happy to help them. These types of people stick to being as self-sufficient as possible.

THE OBSERVER GETS PREOCCUPIED WITH HIS OR HER THOUGHTS AND IMAGINATION. While they are extremely smart, Observers have trouble taking the information that they acquire and put it into action even though they are usually very organized in the accumulation of that information. Observers tend to neglect the needs of their bodies, hearts, and spirits because they focus so much of their energy mentally. In their never-ending quest for seeking more information, they sometimes do not apply that knowledge into action and therefore, miss out on a lot of life experiences.

THE OBSERVER IS EMOTIONALLY DISTANT. Observers tend to be comfortable in the realm of thought and so, they are much less connected when dealing with emotions. Therefore, they often have a difficult time handling the demands of relationships and tend to shy away from forming deep connections. They do so because of their sensitivity and feel like they cannot handle the demands of that relationship. This can lead to loneliness. To compensate for this, they often adopt an attitude of intellectual arrogance or careless indifference. While this helps them cope, it often creates an emotional distance between themselves and others and this distance is often not easily bridged. When they do manage to form deep and meaningful connections with others, type 5s tend to keep lifelong relationships. Even though type 5s have a hard time emotionally expressing themselves, they feel deeply. Because of the deep need for privacy and a fear of intrusion, not many people are aware of the fact that they have so much going on beneath the surface. As a result of this, type 5s tend to have a very minimalistic lifestyle so that their exchange with others and the outside world are kept to a minimum.

THE OBSERVER IS INSECURE. The Observer's need to seek knowledge is often driven by the fact that they feel as if they are ill-equipped to function successfully in the world. They feel inferior in their abilities to do things as well as other people do. Rather than facing this fear, they retreat into their minds. They trick themselves into believing that they can figure things out mentally then rejoin the world better equipped.

How Observers Relate to Other Personality Types

Observers vs. Type 1s

Please see Chapter 2: How Reformers Relate to Other Personality Types: Reformers vs. Type 5s.

Observers vs. Type 2s

Please see Chapter 3: How Helpers Relate to Other Personality Types: Helpers vs. Type 5s.

Observers vs. Type 3s

Please see Chapter 4: How Performers Relate to Other Personality Types: Performers vs. Type 5s.

Observers vs. Types 4s

Please see Chapter 5: How Artists Relate to Other Personality Types: Artists vs. Type 5s.

Observers vs. Types 6s

Both of these personality types are mental types and value accuracy, objectivity, attention to detail, and ability to analyze situations without being biased. The Observer is the more emotionally calm personality type while type 6s are more sympathetic and look for authority in the Observer. The Loyalist's dedication and loyalty can break through the Observer's tendency to isolate his or herself. Potential problems can arise because although both these personality types are mentally inclined, they think differently. Often times this means that they end up on opposite ends of the fence, which can lead to a breakdown in communication and trust.

Observers vs. Types 7s

Both of these personality types are thinking types and have an appreciation for bringing ideas to the relationship. The Observer brings insight, objectivity, and clarity of observation to the relationship and type 7s can bring the enthusiasm for life and spontaneity that the Observer needs to come out of his or her shell. As a result of the tendency of type 5s to emotionally retreat in times of stress, problems may arise because when the pressure rises, type 7s do the opposite and go into hyperdrive and become more emotional. These different coping mechanisms of handling emotional stimuli can cause a rift in the relationship.

Observers vs. Types 8s

A pairing of these two personality types is complementary because they help boost each other's strengths while compensating for each other's weaknesses. Type 8s need to be more self-aware and thoughtful of the impact of their actions on themselves and others, while type 5s need to be more in tune with their bodies and with their environment. The two personality types help balance each other out in a healthy relationship. Both of these personality types are sensitive to rejection and feel rejected easily, which can cause an immediate problem in the relationship. Also, both personality types can be cynical, which can lead to a breakdown in communication.

Observers vs. Types 9s

A relationship between these two personality types can work very effectively because they respect each other's independent nature and allow for both emotional and personal space. Neither is intrusive or hovering. Such a relationship is characterized by respect for each other's boundaries, individuality, and non-intrusiveness. However, there can be too much space between the two personality types, which can cause them to grow apart.

How the Observer Can Improve His or Her Life

This personality type needs to get out of their head and put in the effort to be more intune with their emotional, spiritual, and physical being. They need to realize that making connections with people, engaging in emotional experiences, and stepping out of their heads can make life more enjoyable.

Yoga is a great way to get in touch with your emotions. A great pose to achieve this is called the Child's pose. To achieve this pose, kneel on the floor, sit on your heels, and allow your big toes to touch. With an exhale, lay your torso between your thighs and allow your tailbone to lengthen while you lift the base of your skull away from the back of your neck. Lay your hands on the floor alongside your torso with your thumbs facing up. Rest in this pose for at least 30 seconds and allow your mind to empty itself out. Breathe in and out deeply and feel each breath flow through your body.

Chakra meditations that this personality type can engage in to become more grounded in the present moment and to become more in touch with their emotions includes root chakra, sacral chakra, navel chakra, and heart chakra. Acupressure is also helpful. In addition to the stimulation of the point SP-6 and ST-36, the points TB-5 and KI-6 can be stimulated by an acupressure practitioner. TB-5 can be stimulated to increase sensitivity to feelings and emotions. It is located in the top side of the arm just below the crease of the wrist. KI-6 decreases the effects of fear on the body and is located on the inside of the foot, just below the ankle bone.

Other ways that the Observer can improve their lives include:

● Learning to notice when your mental functioning takes you away from experiencing a moment.

- Staying connected in the present.

- Using exercise as a way to channel nervous energy.

- Not using escapist techniques such as using drugs and alcohol to relax or unwind.

- Taking more decisive actions so that you can increase your self-confidence and self-esteem.

- Learning to cope with conflict by not emotionally withdrawing but by finding healthy solutions.

- Taking the time to become more social and build connections with others.

- Learning to trust in other people by occasionally taking helpful advice so that you can gain a fresh perspective on situations.

Chapter 14: Effective Employment

It is nearly 2020 and a job is often not just a job. It is an extension of our passion

and even ourselves. There are endless degrees, certifications, and experiences we

can build on to create the perfect career. It takes work, effort and dedication. What

we do for ourselves, though, is only half of the equation. Organizations have the

other half. Businesses have the ability to offer an environment where employees

thrive.

We will now discuss the groups that support a great organization and build on

employees' professional desires.

1) CAREER DEVELOPMENT- This factor is connected to the needs for security. This

may be especially important for those (types 5, 6, & 7) in the Intellectual

Center whose driving force is fear. Mentorship and career pathing opportunities are being connected with higher levels of job fulfilment, productivity, professionalism, management skills, and retention. Advancement potential appeals to our more basic needs while compensation may be an outlying attraction. Adequate training is essential to reducing employee turnover.

2) MEANINGFUL WORK- Unhappiness in one's job can be due to several factors such as poor relationships, job content and a misunderstanding of expectations. Types 2, 3 and 4 will most likely be affected by uncertainties in these areas. If there is discontent between what an individual believes their job should be and what they actually experience, dissatisfaction is likely to occur. Therefore, stimulating work, a supportive atmosphere and

role clarity is vital. Individuals want to do work that enhances their life interests. We want to enjoy work as much as we enjoy life, even in difficult times.

3) Organizational Culture and Reputation- EMPLOYEES WHO WISH TO BE connected to a business because of its reputation and culture show their complex need for attachment and success. The Inherent (types 8, 9, and 1), controlled by rage, enjoy social status. Culture and reputation identifies how an organization is involved in the community, diversity in the workplace, their effect on the environment, and employee satisfaction. Therefore, The Inherent may be more attracted to an organization based on their higher-level desires. In contrast, someone that needs income may not be as concerned with social responsibilities.

4) ACKNOWLEDGMENT-Research shows that organizational durability is connected to how well an employee identifies with them and their employer's importance in their life. Individuals are also drawn to more challenging positions as well. Also, employees who are rooted in a business due to both work and non-work impacts are more likely to remain than their counterparts. Studies also support the idea that organizational commitment is relative to employee commitment.

5) LEADERSHIP SUPPORT-Moms are in the workplace much more often in recent decades. There is also an uptick in non-traditional families. It is imperative that organizations recognize that times are changing, employees are changing and expectations may need to be more flexible. With that in mind, we now have the Family Medical Leave Act, Flexible Schedules, et cetera.

Individuals want to their "work" to work with them. Supportive supervisors

make life easier. When you have the ability to communicate your needs and

your company can analyze theirs, it is easier to find a "fit."

6) POSITIVE EMPLOYMENT PROCESSES- Businesses have learned that it is

important to not only discuss the positive aspects of a position they are

hiring for, but also address the negative. This way, everyone at the table

knows what to expect and the employee will be more likely to stay.

7) Competitive, Skills-Based Compensation and Benefits- EMPLOYERS USE A

variety of ways to entice employees. Some have incentive plans with

attainable, measurable goals while others may use market surveys.

Compensation market surveys provide valuable insight using regional, educational and job specific information to determine a competitive salary base.

Businesses are a lot like people. You can apply the Enneagram to identify strengths and weaknesses, thereby, identifying areas of focus for improvement. In doing so, organizations can increase employee retention, improve processes and build on a great foundation.

Chapter 15: The Investigator

Synopsis

Whether they are Sherlock Holmes is other than the point. These individuals are the world class scholars of society – you can simply depend on them to issue you a profound examination on a subject!

This part discusses:

• What an agent is about

• Why are agents great to have around

• What is most troublesome about agents

• Dealing with them and drawing out the best

• Who they coexist with

• Who they don't alongside

Their mission for learning is praiseworthy! Express gratitude toward God for agents, generally our reality will be drained of point by point information!

What Is An Investigator?

An agent, is a kind of mastermind who preferences to take a rearward sitting arrangement, watch the circumstance, make all the expository contemplations for the best choices and returns after a full investigation of the circumstance is carried out.

They commonly don't impart their passionate state to others as they keep down regularly discovering security in their psyches where they can withdraw and strategize, just to rise later with full certainty!

You can simply rely on them to give canny answers, and when they are occupied with something, they have a tendency to wind up truly well perused and learned around there.

They are likewise a bit timid yet more free (or hesitant to acknowledge help) wanting to accomplish things all alone actually when other individuals are more than willing to give help.

The Good

To the specialist, learning vanquishs all — on the grounds that their heavenly thought is in light of omniscience. Their fundamental yearning is to be capable in all that they attempt, feeling ahead regarding information and comprehension.

They are great at candidly confining themselves regarding the matter of taking care of rationally difficult assignments, experiencing a lot of study and exploration till no closures — awesome on the off chance that you truly need to get down into point of interest over a complex subject.

The Bad

Examiners have a tendency to be over systematic — thus the term... loss of motion by investigation.

They are frequently extremely closefisted individuals too, not willing to impart past their limits of security and solace. Due to their 'know-all' disposition, they have a tendency to be standoffish others regularly getting to be exceptionally pretentious and judgmental believing that other individuals will never comprehend or realize a better way.

On occasion, their mission for learning and comprehension will make them very rapacious and covetous for all the more where it counts. Their "thirst" will never be fulfilled and the most exceedingly bad part is, they don't candidly express this.

Instructions to Deal With Them

Where it counts inside, agents are delicate individuals and truly limitation in the matter of passionate statement.

At the point when managing insurance toward oneself examiners, don't ask about their mystery musings or profound exploration. They will feel that you won't comprehend them at any rate and it is exceedingly nosy of their security.

At the point when managing sexual examiners, it can be an exceptionally complex correspondence process for sure. One reason is on the grounds that they are bad at conveying their inward sentiments, yet they long to impart their seeing on specific themes to their accomplices profoundly.

The best thing you can do is to attempt and meet them midway and research on the subject all around ok to have a canny discussion with them.

To wrap things up are the social agents – the swarm will need to endure with their social haughtiness, needing to set up to their long speculations (and once in a while tedious, exhausting ones) yet attempt and seem intrigued sufficiently long to issue them affirmation of their extraordinary comprehension and you'll do fine with them.

They work exceptionally well with challengers (sort 8) who are frequently pushes them to push their limits of omniscience and they despise being around aficionados (sort 7) whose energetic nature turns off the melancholic agents with their mindless fun and excitement.

Chapter 16: Type Five Personality

TYPE FIVE (investigator and observer) - As an investigator, Type Five personalities are motivated by the need to 'know and understand' the world around them. As an observer, their five senses (including the sixth) are constantly tuned to picking up the tiniest of signals that could open a door to knowledge and insight.

The characteristics of Type Fives are as follows -

- Type Five personality individuals want to be seen as knowledgeable and capable individuals who know everything about something and something about everything. Having a desire to always be in the know pushes them to the limits of educational attainment. This trait can also be seen in Type Fives whose careers do not require a lot of formal education, they still want to know all they can about their chosen profession or occupation. They would rather not take a guess concerning a problem or issue about which they have no prior knowledge.

- Type Fives detest the idea of appearing ignorant or foolish in a public setting. Occasionally when overtaken by pride, they may want to dazzle others with their knowledge of a particular topic or subject. But when the tables turn and they know little or nothing about a subject, they would rather remain quiet than look foolish in the eyes of others. If they choose to talk, they may be observed asking too many questions than normal and trying to know as much as they can.

- Being part of the mental or thinking group, Type Fives prefer to take a cerebral approach to whatever challenges or problems they are tackling. And this is why they may struggle in tackling issues that require a certain level of creativity and out-of-the-box thinking. They are often obsessed with being factual and objective when making decisions or drawing up solutions and may not be willing to try novel ideas unless they have been successfully used elsewhere.

- Individuals with Type Five personality are highly analytical beings and would favour the cold hard facts ahead of personal sentiments or bias. When they are faced with a problem or crisis, they start by examining and drawing conclusions from the materiality of the case. They are often methodical in their quest for solutions and answers. Working with people who favour the subjective approach to issues may put them at loggerheads with such people.

- People with Type Five personality have a tendency to be absent-minded especially when thinking about things that are going on around them. Psychological research has shown that this is a notable characteristic of brainy people and many of such people call into the Type Five category. In some cases, they may even be observed soliloquising or talking to themselves about an issue or problem for which they are yet to find a workable solution.

- Type Fives may prefer to search out the root causes of problems and proffer solutions without actually getting involved in the implementation of the solutions. Having done the mental work, they want to leave the physically-demanding aspect for others to execute. They prefer to work with their minds and not their muscles or allow their brains to work rather than their biceps. Without a proper understanding of this, they might be wrongly judged as being lazy and indolent.

- People with Type Five personality are usually open-minded and willing to learn new things. This makes them good listeners when communicating with people. They want to continuously increase in knowledge and learning and are attracted to people from they can learn a thing or two. When they show signs of being garrulous, the only thing that can get them to listen is a voice that is spewing out useful knowledge or information.

- Type Five individuals do not really crave attention from others unless such attention cannot be avoided in any way. Drawing attention to themselves may sometimes become inevitable when others are attracted to them by virtue of admiring their vast amount of knowledge. A Type Five personality is not a showbiz type even though being a specialist or expert has the potential of making them popular in their domains of influence.

Below is a list of renowned Type Five personalities in human history -

- NEIL ARMSTRONG - An American astronaut and aeronautical engineer who was the first person to walk on the moon. He was also a naval aviator, test pilot and university professor. He was awarded the Presidential Medal of Freedom and the Congressional Space Medal of Honour on different occasions. Neil Armstrong's love for aviation and space technology was ignited as a little boy when his father took him to the Cleveland Air Races and by the age of sixteen, he had earned a student flight certificate. By the age of seventeen, he had started studying aeronautical engineering at Purdue University. His interest and love for understanding airspace technology could only grow at this stage, which were signs of his Type Five personality.

- BILL GATES - An American business magnate and principal founder of Microsoft Corporation. He is regarded as one of the best-known entrepreneurs of the personal computer revolution and presently engages in philanthropic endeavours around the world. As a Type Five, Bill Gates was a perfect example of an iconoclast who felt that he didn't have to complete his college degree before he could realise his dreams. Also, he took an interest in computer programming as a teenager and was excused from math classes to pursue his interest. He wrote his very first computer program around this time too.

- STEPHEN HAWKING - An English theoretical physicist and author who achieved commercial success with several works of popular science in which he discusses his own theories. Aside from the numerous awards he has received in his career, he has also being awarded the Presidential Medal of Freedom. He was not initially successful in academic terms when he was in high school but after a while, he began to show considerable aptitude for scientific subjects. With the help of his high school mathematics teacher, Stephen Hawking and some close friends built a computer from clock parts, telephone switchboard and other recycled components.

- ALBERT EINSTEIN - A German theoretical physicist who developed the theory of relativity, one of the two pillars of modern physics (alongside quantum mechanics). He received the Nobel Prize in Physics in 1921 and he made significant contribution to the philosophy of science. He published more than 300 scientific papers and more than 150 non-scientific works and his intellectual achievements have made his name synonymous with the term 'genius.' It is quite difficult to find another individual with more Type Five characteristics than Albert Einstein. At the beginning of his career, he thought that Newtonian mechanics was no longer sufficient to reconcile the laws of classical mechanics with the laws of the electromagnetic field and this led him to develop his special theory of relativity.

- ROBERT DE NIRO - An American actor, producer and director who works includes films that are considered the greatest and most influential on a global scale. He is the recipient of various accolades and awards including the Presidential Medal of Freedom. One of the directors (Elia Kazan) who worked closely with Robert De Niro described him as someone who was very meticulous, imaginative and precise. He went further to say Robert De Niro would figure everything out both inside and outside and calculates almost everything he does in a good way. He had a habit of immersing himself completely into any movie role that he wanted to portray. At various times in his career, he has done strange things to prepare himself for an imminent role in the movies. Examples include taking up a job as a taxi driver for a few weeks, learning to play saxophone and learning to box in the ring.

- BOBBY FISCHER - An American chess grandmaster and the eleventh World Chess Champion who many consider the 'greatest chess player' of all time. He became the United States Chess Champion and took part in the World Championship in his teenage years. He made numerous lasting contributions to chess including a patented chess timing system and a another variant of chess known as Fischerandom. As a Type Five, his exceptional level of intelligence was already evident as a teenage prodigy. At a tender age, when other family members refused to play chess with him, he would play the game against himself. As an adolescent, he had already joined the strongest chess club in the country

- ALAN GREENSPAN - An American economist who served as Chairman of the Federal Reserve of the United States from 1987 to 2006, he served in this position under the regime of four successive United States presidents. His father worked as a stockbroker and market analyst in New York and this may have had an impact on his choice of career. As a logical positivist, he believed that only things that are verifiable through empirical observations can be considered as cognitively meaningful.

- ALFRED HITCHCOCK - An English film director and producer who is widely regarded as one of the most influential filmmakers in the history of cinema. Over a period of six decades, he directed over fifty feature films and was referred to as the 'Master of Suspense.' He was knighted in 1979, some months before his death. Alfred Hitchcock attended Jesuit Grammar School where he was reported to have developed his organisational and analytical abilities. His Type Five nature made him to inform his parents about his desire to study engineering in his teens and after a short while, started taking night classes at the London County Council School of Engineering and Navigation. His analytical background play a role in developing a movie making technique known as the 'Hitchcockian style' which involved using a camera to imitate a person's gaze and framing shots to maximise anxiety and fear. A film critic said that the real meaning of a Hitchcock film is in the method and that it is an organism, with the whole implied in every detail and every detail related to the whole.

The typical roles played by Type Fives include -

- THE ANALYST - A Type Five personality would want to drill deep into issues instead of just scratching the surface. They want to unravel what the average person cannot perceive or decipher. They are willing to use any kind of tool, strategy or technique available to get to the bottom of the matter.

- THE BACKROOM BOY - Type Fives would also readily take up the role of a backroom boy which allows them to offer expert advice and counsel without having an official status or position within an organisation or any other formal setup. Having a Type Five as a close friend or partner can be very helpful in handling problems that exceed your capacity and expertise.

- THE COMPUTER GEEK - Without doubt, a Type Five personality could be a computer geek but the use of this term is figurative and describes the nerd tendencies of Type Fives. They can produce ideas and solutions that enable us solve tough problems and interestingly such solutions may not be difficult for them to find.

- THE PROBLEM- SOLVER - Type Fives are not scared by the size of a problem especially one that can be solved using human knowledge. They love to be acknowledged as the individual who brought a practicable solution to the table.

In their spare time, they may even be ruminating about problems that are not within their domain of influence.

- THE SPY - Jobs relating to intelligence gathering or espionage will fit a Type Five personality. Gathering and analysing relevant information about people and activities in a covert manner is not an overly difficult task for this kind of Enneagram personality.

- THE SCIENTIST - Type Fives like to rely on facts as a basis for their judgement and decisions and would be quick to criticise decisions that are based on bias or prejudice. More often than not, they are systematic in the way they examine and analyse issues and problems. Therefore, working as a scientist, engineer or researcher in many fields is a natural habitat for them.

- THE BOFFIN - A boffin is a scientist or technician engaged in military research and therefore this role is not very different from the preceding one. Being a boffin also implies that Type Fives can function in a well-ordered and regulated environment like a large corporation or the armed forces.

● THE PUNDIT - A pundit is a learned person in a particular discipline or someone who has been admitted into membership in a scholarly field. Type Fives love to learn all they can about an area of interest and would not have much difficulty stepping into the shoes of a pundit.

● THE ICONOCLAST - An iconoclast is someone who attacks well-established and cherished ideas or traditional institutions. A Type Five would no doubt become iconoclastic if he or she considers such ideals and institutions to be based on fallacy and superstitious beliefs.

● THE EXPERT - Being an expert in a particular field of endeavour gives Type Fives an opportunity to showcase his talents and gifts which is something they love to do. They would willingly share specialist knowledge with others even without asking for anything in return.

Type Fives usually have a high level of proficiency in decision making, problem solving and analytical thinking. They have the ability to see the big picture and also the minute details behind it all. Being curious can help them discover and define what was hitherto vague and confounding but this attribute may also get them into trouble sometimes when they become too inquisitive. Their positive qualities include being sensitive, analytical, trustworthy, objective, self-contained and persevering and their negative qualities include being arrogant, stingy, pessimistic, unassertive, distant and critical.

The following careers would suit a Type Five personality - STEM-related careers (science, technology, engineering and mathematics), arts (writing and music), finance, military or civil intelligence and academia.

In this chapter, we have examined the following -

•The characteristic features of Type Five personalities

- Famous Type Five personalities in history
- Typical roles that can be played by a Type Five personality

Chapter 17: Type Eight: The In-Charge Caregiver

In This Chapter:

Live and let live? I don't think so

The generator - step aside, I'm energized
Be reasonable - do it my way!

In charge on the outside, insecure inside
Sorry! I didn't mean to step on you

Identifying the Eight in Yourself and Others

Eights are one of the easier types to spot, especially the Eight with the Seven wing. Eights are strong, opinionated, often jovial, and can use language that tends to startle or bypass the norm. Your energy is bigger than most people's and you take charge easily.

Nonverbal cues

Eights can show their independence in dress, actions, or beliefs. Eights are not hiding or trying to create an image to please people. It is more of a take-it-or-leave-it attitude. Eights can speak bluntly and might not realize how others will be affected. Practical jokes are fine with Eights, particularly if they are initiating them!

Eight's Non-verbal cues include:

Handling challenge and confrontation.

Taking on leadership roles easily - whether voted in or not! Living full tilt - play hard, work hard, go after what they want. Having a commanding presence, big builds, with strong torsos. Having a good belly laugh.

verbal cues

Eights love to talk about subjects most people don't touch—sex, politics, and religion—and are willing to disagree with others. Sometimes you challenge just to test. Not much is forbidden, if it creates a rise or the truth out of people. You like language that affects.

Verbal cues can include:

Willingness to complain to a manager or owner. Having a hard time filtering what they say.

Sharing opinions as facts. Saying "no" easily.

Talking in a strong or aggressive tone but with a teddy-bear heart.

Use of aggressive words (often for fun or startle quality) such as "kill, destroy, demolish, slap, choke, push." Curse words are not unusual

Eights in Caregiving

Eights can light up a city with their drive for doing, but they are short on patience, so what you see is what you get. The most body-instinctive type, Eights tend not to take no for an answer. If there's an obstacle in the way slowing down progress, call an Eight to blow it away. For the Eight caregiver, there are periods when she shines at getting results, but slower times and relationship difficulties sorely challenge her.

Preferring action to inaction, and driven by impulse, these take- charge people have energy to burn and can't stand to wait. No brakes, please! Eights easily feel controlled and are on the alert for that possibility. The limitations of caregiving can drive them crazy. Quick to take on the healthcare establishment, they go for the green light and take charge, so that others can't take charge of them. If you test family and medical professionals the way you'd test a new car and push your agenda hard, you likely are an Eight.

From your perspective, Charles Darwin was right—life (and caregiving) is a struggle for survival in which only the fittest prevail. An Eight caregiver's strength is power. You do whatever it takes to be strong or at least project strength. You hide any weakness, for fear others will take advantage. Present a forceful front to family, drive through the caretaking issues, and you have a chance of surviving this journey. If you're tough with others and yourself, you can manage. To protect and advocate for your Loved

One, you feel you have to constantly prove, challenge, and confront. You even like conflict, if it brings out the truth. You want everything brought to the surface.

You tend to rebel. You are the bad boy/bad girl of the Enneagram and don't like to follow unnecessary rules, though you can demand that others follow yours. You want fairness but may treat others unfairly, if you're upset. You shoot from the hip and lip and may only think later. At times you can be unaware of your power to impact others. You're simply trying to get to the truth and are surprised if others pull away from your directness.

Unlike the Six, who mentally challenges, you also physically challenge. You live in your body and are ready to leap, jump, or push, whatever it takes to protect yourself and your Loved One. You live by your instincts and are the most purely physical of all the types.

You pull your own weight, and so should everyone else! You don't like insecurity, doubt, fear, or weakness. If your Loved

One or a family member is timid it drives you a little crazy. Open on one hand, guarded on another, you usually are generous when people are straight with you and particularly need help. But if others are shirking responsibility or taking advantage of you, you tend to be dismissive or confrontational.

Eight's Positive Traits

Your energy generally knows no limits, and neither do your plans, dreams, and schemes. Your hard work makes them happen so aspects of caregiving can go smoothly for you and your Loved One. Subtlety is not a game you play. Everyone knows who they're dealing with—what you see is what you get.

You inspire others. You're not a talker, but a doer. Why put things off ? You'll do anything for your Loved One's health and well-being and it is decisive action that makes it happen. Geared for action and focused on results, you don't let anything get in your way.

You are generous. When your Loved One is in trouble, you'll give anything to help. You protect the vulnerable and fight for justice and freedom. You watch out for bullies and face them. You're the one who speaks up in the nursing home or family meeting, and your honesty is either a breath of fresh air or a hurricane—with you, there's no middle ground.

You are independent, trusting your own decisions and not needing approval before acting. Self-motivated, you accept that life is tough and you're ready, either alone or on a team, to withstand an enemy, troubles, or storms.

Positive caregiving traits of Eights include: Being direct and clear

Trusting your instinct

Maintaining a leadership orientation Being passionate and energized Being in charge of life

Able to face conflict and challenge

Eight's Challenges

Anger is far easier for you than is acknowledging and expressing your insecurities. When you are sad, afraid, stressed, or guilty, it is likely to come out as anger. Anger can arise from not getting what you want, feeling held back, or being misunderstood. It is relieved when you express it or get what you want.

Self-expression makes you feel powerful, and you are powerful, though you also hide your feelings of powerlessness even from yourself. You don't realize that insecurity, doubt and mixed feelings are natural and have a place. Since you are as insecure and afraid as the next person, why spend so much time and effort hiding it? If you share yourself, most people won't reject you—they will trust you more, allowing you to be more effective. Your family can operate as more of a team. You will be able to relax while exerting less control. You will feel less alone and better understood.

Too-quick action can cause blunders requiring damage control. You can overstep, violating your Loved One's basic right to manage her/ his life, or damaging your relationships. Your skill for taking action can actually slow down positive change. You make things happen too much from pushing, pure effort and daunting relentlessness, yet don't always know the power of listening, letting go, empathy, creating alliances, and letting things build at a natural pace. Be open to different ways and options that others may reveal to you.

Instead of trusting to a natural unfolding of events and believing people will support you and accept you, you tend to overprotect and control - just in case! You tend to feel it is better to take charge and make the first move than to be on the receiving end. You sometimes think the worst, in regard to people's motivations, yet you're open to the good, when you see it. People give in to you, at times because they are afraid or overwhelmed by your drive, or because it may take too much effort to fight you. You bank on that, but why have a fighting stance in the first place? Go with what works more than having to win, control, or be right. A little compromise can go a long way. Everyone can win. This is caregiving, as in giving care. You need to take care when giving care. Focus on cooperation more than contention.

With your automatic action persona and your suit of armor, it is

hard for even you to know your own needs and desires. What really is your deeper truth? Are you fulfilling your true needs? Refocus on your personal goals, not just your first impulse. You may fight the good fight, but make sure it is a fight from which you can get good outcomes. Fighting may pump you up or give you a boost, but is it the energy you ultimately want? Is that your best result?

Eight's most challenging traits include: Uncontrolled anger and bluntness Lack of impulse control

Not following rules you make for others Taking charge when others need to lead

Taking action when waiting is required
Control at the expense of teamwork

Personal Growth for Eights

Eights grow by counting to 100 and slowing down their actions and expressions. It is great to speak up and also good to hold back at times, quite a challenge for you, who often feels sure. Your confidence is wonderful and don't let it hide the parts of yourself that are sensitive and uncertain. You can show it all. For Eights to grow, take these steps:

Be powerful but gentle - You are powerful and a model for directness and action. Sometimes, though, you come on too strongly and scare people away. Be gentler in your strength. Slow down, lower your voice, and connect to where others are, not just where you want them to be. Have compassion for their process, apart from what you think they should do. Get feedback from others as to how they experience you. Learn if you are balancing your strong presence with gentleness.

See others as different - Of course you notice differences, but you tend to think others should think and act as you do. Everyone is an individual with a very different life process. When they act or think differently from you, they are not betraying you. Revenge is not appropriate. You don't have all the answers for how others or the world should be. Ask others if they feel you are relating to them personally or are being controlling, and let go, when you are trying to control.

Don't overdo - You tend to eat, drink, and be merry; overworking; overplaying; overextending yourself. Find the right balance for you. Notice tendencies to not get enough sleep or have too much indulgence, with consequences that might not be worth it. Keep a log of your activities and set some limits for yourself. It is good to know your limits.

Be sensitive to others - You love honesty and say or blurt out what you think. Honesty needs to be tempered with sensitivity. Comments need to be measured for consequences. Statements that poke fun at others or highlight their weaknesses may hurt people. Be selective in your joking. People will avoid you, if they perceive you as too gruff for their taste.

Show your vulnerable side - You aren't as tough as you look. The more you show some of your insecurity, fear, doubt, weakness, and vulnerability, the more others will trust you. Others will feel safer with you, when you aren't so overly confident and cocky. Most people will accept you more and know you've been afraid to expose your softer side. Think of times when you have done this and people accepted you. Vow to do this even more, in the right circumstances

Be a follower - You are a natural leader, but don't feel you have to take charge every time. Just let the process unfold. Others may need to lead in their own style and you might take that opportunity away, if you take over too quickly. Be part of the gang, without having to lead it. Offer some advice, but don't think you're always right. Be more in the middle and less dominant, when necessity isn't calling you to be in charge.

Temper your anger - You tend to express anger easily. Realize that your anger might be masking feelings like hurt, fear, pain or sadness. Be in touch with that softer and more vulnerable side. You are as sweet as you are tough, so let that side of you show more. If people remember your quick anger, they may hold back from showing you parts of themselves, to your loss. Don't expect others to be as direct as you can be. It is just not in their nature. Ask others how they feel about your anger. Risk sharing what's behind it.

The Eight's Heart, Soul, and Mind

Eights in Relationships

You can be wonderful in relationship, as you are full of life, create all manner of positive things in the world, and don't accept excuses for why things can't happen or change. You challenge others to act, be courageous, and don't take no for an answer. You support a can-do spirit and don't like whining, helplessness, or depression. All of this can be a great support for your Loved One.

Relationships are important to you but also a bit scary. You like people and can be loyal, but you hate that relationships bring up fears and insecurities. You struggle with the differences between yourself and others, wishing they could see things your way. You wonder why they are being stubborn, and don't see that the stubborn one is you!

When there is conflict in your family, or between you and your Loved One, you put your all into trying to convince, yet don't easily see your need to compromise. Recognizing the validity of different approaches is essential for your relationship health. It will protect you from others withdrawing from your one-sided views. Especially with the many stakeholders in caregiving, it is best to take a course of negotiation and communication.

You really struggle when others are withdrawn, indirect, or manipulative, and you'll hound them until they speak straight. Realize there are many forces that encourage indirectness, hinting, and roundabout ways of communication that may cause challenge and conflict. There may be valid reasons why others choose a less direct route than you do. Listen first before judging and acting.

Relationship Advice for Eights - Make friends with your fears and insecurities, and share them. Listen to others' points of view. Practice compromise and negotiation. Develop empathy and compassion for others.

Eight's Spiritual Side

Your spirituality finds expression in appreciating that which gives life. You don't back off from life and you appreciate and use what you've been given. Some people ask God for guidance. You do too, but you also realize it is up to you to do the work. You can surrender to a higher force, but barring a bad connection, you realize that higher force is within you. Many Eights do too much alone.

Spiritual growth as an Eight will serve you especially well as a caregiver. Your spiritual growth is to feel part of the whole, instead of controlling the whole. You tend not to trust the flow of events, pushing the timing of things, while more allowance, more tolerance, and awareness of limitations will greatly aid your evolutionary process. When self-aware, you are a model for the family, guiding it toward right action. You inspire and lead while welcoming the participation of others. You protect those who would be misled or hurt by others.

How Eights Think & Make Decisions

You think a lot about protection, control, who has the power, who's trustworthy and what actions need to be taken. You think about what you want and how to get there, and can be derogatory toward those who get in your way. Occasionally you feel guilty for overstepping your bounds. You think about your fears but go right back to solutions and how to be strong.

Eights are decisive, often to the extreme. You trust your first impulse, partially to avoid any wavering thoughts or feelings. You don't like the slightest whiff of ambivalence. You thrive on the extremes of black or white, strong or weak, right or wrong. Any decision is better than no decision! With such compulsive action, Eights can be prone to excesses of eating or drinking.

Eights often decide for others, which obviously can cause conflict. It can also be disempowering for your Loved One. Waiting or being inconvenienced by others doesn't feel comfortable, so you speed things along, running over the slower or indecisive types in the process. You don't know what is best for others, and if you over-control or dominate, you'll either get resistance or anger projected toward you. Ultimately you can fracture the family team.

Eight's inner thoughts may include: Blurting things out gets me in trouble

How could someone not know what they want? It is hard to stop eating.

God, they are slow.

This is the quick and right solution.

Eight's Thought and Action Alternatives

It may seem counter-intuitive, but with less focus on action and results, your caregiving will be more effective while preserving your relationships. Especially at those times when action can cause damage, inaction would better serve you. There are long periods in caregiving when waiting is the better course. A good deal of caretaking teaches patience with the unknown. Later, when decisions are required, or are requested by your Loved One, they will be well thought through. And moderation in eating and drinking will support true health in mind, body, and spirit.

Relationships are the strong threads that hold together the fabric of family and caregiving support. Focus less on your own effectiveness and more on others, making room for their differences and letting them know that they are valued. When working with both your Loved One and your family members, give decision-making support to them or nudge them in your direction. Practice a velvet glove approach rather than pushing.

Thoughts that would better serve Eights include: I apologize. I spoke too hastily.

People are different from me. Not everyone acts on their first impulse.

Let me slow down when I eat and stop before I'm full.

Maybe I can in a nicer way encourage them to get to the point. Let me hear their side. Let's find a compromise here.

Conclusion

Thanks for making it through to the end of this book, let's hope it was informative and able to provide you with all the tools you need to achieve your goals of self-discovery.

The next step is to study your types. Study your core type, your wing type, your security point type, and your stress point type. While it is important to avoid labeling those around you, it's also important to study how your type interacts with others. Understanding how each type interacts with others can help you understand other people's behavior. Utilize the information regarding relationships between Enneagram types to develop better ways to approach problems between you and those around you.

www.ingramcontent.com/pod-product-compliance
Lightning Source LLC
Chambersburg PA
CBHW072002070526
44583CB00015B/1293